The Suza Wedding Feast

A Play in Three Acts

by

András Sütő

the suza wedding feast

~ a play in three acts~

by

András Sütő

Translated by

Csilla Bertha & Donald E. Morse

contents

introduction

Hungarian literature cannot be understood or interpreted without having some knowledge of history. Transylvanian Hungarian literature—the literature of the Hungarian ethnic minority living in what is today Romania—is even more strongly connected to history than that of present-day Hungary due to changes in the minority's status in the twentieth century. Writers, artists, intellectuals undertook the task of becoming the living conscience of their people, especially in periods of dictatorship when no democratic or free institutions existed to ensure human rights of the minorities. Old-fashioned as it may sound, these writers assumed such roles as carrying the responsibility for the community, guarding individual and communal human rights, preserving cultural and moral integrity and identity in the face of dictatorial oppression, *in addition to*, and not instead of, their artistic concerns with aesthetic, intellectual, emotional, and spiritual issues. Thereby they not only interpreted history but also, similarly to the old prophets and vates-poets, contributed to its shaping, through influencing the consciousness of the people. In Romania one such period was the 1960s-1980s when the Hungarian minority's survival was more than ever threatened under the darkest years of the already bleak Nicolae Ceauşescu's dictatorial communist regime.

History plays are one effective way of obliquely dramatizing the current situation of a community. András Sütő's *The Suza Wedding Feast* (written in 1980 and published in 1981), a metaphoric history play, offers a parallel between the plot (taken from

Greek—Macedonian history when Alexander the Great colonized and attempted to totally assimilate Persia and the Persians) and the situation of the Hungarian minority in Romania in the 1970s-80s. Alexander's diabolical plans focus on language and culture: after his military victory over the Persians, he encroaches on the most private feelings of individuals when he orders his governors and soldiers to marry Persian women so that their children to be born will be brought up in Greco-Macedonian culture and language. Sütő affirms that language, the mother tongue, is a stronghold of identity, a storehouse of communal cultural memory, a binding force, for, as the proverbial saying goes: "a nation lives in its language,"[1] to which he adds that "so does any national minority." Sütő argues in *Évek – hazajáró lelkek* [*Years – Returning Ghosts*] (1980) that one's right to language is an obvious human right that it "should not even be declared as such. Yet it is necessary as long as chauvinism... is devouring, among other things, mother tongues."

In *The Suza Wedding Feast* the power of language is vividly emphasized when the Persians are told that "[T]he lord of the world [Alexander] isn't afraid of death, but ... he is afraid of your lullabies. ... Because your language and your religion, as long as you practice them, are treason, betrayal, a continuous conspiracy against us." The conqueror wants, therefore, to deprive the conquered of both but hypocritically tries to hide his real purpose. He pretends to be generous speaking about what he calls "the special joy of the

---

[1] A nineteenth-century proverbial saying attributed to István Széchenyi.

defeated" because in exchange for obedience each conquered person

> receives our gods, the real ones, and the right to speak our language and to observe our ancient customs. It's the generosity of Alexander that—under those conditions—we're ready to absorb anyone whether he be Persian, Scythian, Hindu ..., or any other barbarian. What's more: they can even use our names.

Alexander's cynicism and hypocrisy directly correspond to the oppressive political practices of the Romanian communist dictator. After World War I, Transylvania, an organic part of historical Hungary, was given to neighboring Romania in 1920 after the Paris/Versailles Peace Treaties.[2] The approximately two million Hungarians living there then instantly became the largest ethnic minority in Europe, a minority that has suffered different degrees and levels of cultural genocide including attacks on the mother tongue in the form of closing Hungarian schools, disappearing archives, even re-inscribing old tombstones in cemeteries—to create evidence that Romanians were the more ancient inhabitants of the land. After World War II, the double oppression of the communist regime and the chauvinism of the majority nation, culminating in Ceauşescu's tyranny and self-deification, made it more and more difficult yet more and more necessary to write about contemporary atrocities. Sütő was one of the most prominent prose writers and playwrights who consistently went on fighting

---

[2] Other parts of Hungary were given to other neighboring countries, resulting in the loss of two thirds of Hungarian territory.

for basic human rights.[3] For that he—along with several other writers—often resorted to parabolic, metaphorical expression which necessitates that readers and subsequent audiences read between and behind the lines. Sütő interrogated the relationship between political power and the conscientious individual, and among forms of behavior, ways of resistance and possibilities of survival especially in his "Trilogy": *The Palm Sunday of a Horse Dealer* (1975), *Star on the Stake* (1975) and *Cain and Abel* (1977) as well as in novels and essays.[4]

The Suza Wedding Feast, with its epic plot—built not on one central dilemma or an individual hero's conflict but on continuous and many-threaded conflicts between and within communities—may sound initially rather undramatic yet it inexorably creates a special kind of tragedy. In *The Death of Tragedy*, George Steiner asserts that the process of tragedy's disappearance as a genre began at the turn of the eighteenth—nineteenth centuries when theatre-

---

[3] Sütő's works were banned in Romania after 1980, and he was able to publish them only in Hungary until 1989 when the communist regime in Romania collapsed. *The Suza Wedding Feast*'s performance at Kolozsvár (Cluj-Napoca) in 1981 was the last of his plays to be performed in Romania for a decade. Also, the scheduled performance of *The Suza Wedding Feast* in Marosvásárhely [Tîrgu-Mureş] where he lived, was banned. Sütő and his family were under constant surveillance and harassed by the Secret Police, the fearful "Securitate." Nevertheless, after the fall of communism in 1990, an organized Romanian ultra-nationalist mob attacked and beat him gouging out his eye. His wounds were to lead to his death a few years later

[4] Sütő also wrote several memoranda and protests against the destruction of his minority group and for human and community rights; some of these circulated abroad—an especially dangerous service then.

going ceased to be a communal experience, a ritual. Tragedy in Western cultures consists in the moral (Greek, Shakespearean) or psychological (American) fall of the hero or, in modern drama, the tragic alienation of the hero from his own or his society's values. In small countries suffering from external oppression, however, communal feelings survived much longer than in happier, independent countries and very often in their literature and especially in drama the irreparable loss is *not only* individual and generally human but also and most emphatically that of the national, ethnic, religious community. Within that frame, such plays usually investigate forms of behavior in the conflicting groups and search for possibilities of preserving moral integrity in the face of any insane tyranny. Often the hero fails not because s/he would be alienated from society's values, as in many modern plays, but on the contrary, because s/he desperately strives under oppression to preserve them against all odds. The emphasis on the moral values and their realization is still central but is seen in relation to existential questions of individual and community survival.

Plenty of moral and psychological dilemmas plague the individuals in Sütő's play, yet the drama focuses on a tragic communal loss without the restoration of the world order afterwards, and in spite of the sacrifice of the hero. More exactly: individual and communal losses are so closely interrelated that it is needless or impossible to separate them. As another Transylvanian-Hungarian writer, Géza Páskándi (1933–1995) asserts in an open letter to Václav Havel, it is necessary to defend not only what is obvious such as individual human rights, but in addition, what may be less obvious, that is, the ethnic or national minority's rights. Páskándi further emphasizes the indivisibility of individual and communal rights and the absurdity of such divisions. As members of the oppressed Hungarian national minority whose mother tongue's very existence and survival was endangered, Sütő and Páskándi suffered from a double oppression: something which most other Central Europeans playwrights, such as Sławomir Mrożek in Poland and Havel in the Czech Republic (then Czechoslovakia) did not encounter, although they, too, cried out against oppression. In that respect, a closer parallel may be found in Irish plays since the Irish are still sensitive to the loss of their mother tongue, dramatized by, among others, the best-known contemporary Irish playwright, Brian Friel in *Translations*.[5]

Tragedy is omnipresent in *The Suza Wedding Feast*. The conflict-system present in the basic situation is manifold and complex, made up of several branching-off relationships that fortify each other, which further emphasizes the wide-spread nature of colonization's effects and the whole community's endangerment. Which, in turn, limits the individual's capacity to follow his/her own inner moral or emotional drives. Sütő problematizes the relation between the individual and the community. When the ancient, organic forms of mutual interdependence between individual and community become distorted, when order is violently turned upside down (for instance, due to colonization from outside and/or tyranny introduced inside), the individual loses freedom of choice and the community disintegrates. The plural "you" and "us" becomes an expression of hostility,

---

[5] Incidentally, written in the same year as *The Suza Wedding Feast*.

and there is no longer trust—as the Persians "entrusted" Betis, their leader "with the use of the plural" when they asked him to pray for them— human relationships, friendship, love, loyalty become compromised or broken amongst the millstones of uncontrolled and uncontrollable oppressive power. While psychological distortions and moral failures are shown as consequences of the inhuman situation, Sütő does not romanticize the defeated, but instead shows human weaknesses leading to servility and self-betrayal often with sarcasm, sometimes with empathy, but always with the many shades in-between.

The greatest despair occurs among those colonized Persians who resist forced assimilation, when they become aware of their compatriots' betrayal thanks to the intimidation, bribery or false promises of the colonizers. For instance, in response to one of Alexander's diabolically cynical measures to encourage the conquered to humiliate themselves, Persian fathers bring their daughters to marry the Greeks in the hope of a tax-reduction. Such diversions upend the community itself and at the same time deprive individuals of their sense of belonging, old values, and fixed points of orientation as several examples in *The Suza Wedding Feast* make clear (such as, Bessos's schizophrenic murderous act or Suzia's going mad). The plight of the central hero and heroine—the Greek Parmenion and the Persian Eanna—centers on how their efforts to reconcile private and communal commitments and attractions are doomed to failure and lead to tragedy given the colonial situation. In the most poetic parts of the play, they strive to shed the hostility between the plural "you" and "us" and together seek their private escape into an "inhabitable dream," where they could live in peace and forget about the world. Inevitably this must remain a pious wish, for there is no such solution, no such escape.

The colonial situation, made more unbearable by Alexander's individual tyranny, corrupts people on both sides. The Greek governors became demoralized in their fear of, and in the "horse-race" for the favors of the unpredictable ruler as it becomes important "to be the last to exit from him" with his last instructions; human relations become impossible as a consequence of the introduction of informing on one another.[6] Only Parmenion, the childhood friend of Alexander and now one of his governors in Suza, stands apart with his moral standards, honesty and doubts from the power-hungry and lust-driven Greek leaders. His love for the beautiful Persian Eanna partly opens his eyes to the bestiality of the Greeks in Persia, and Eanna in turn, tries to see him as the person he is, instead of as the conqueror. Parmenion, while differing from the majority of his compatriots and sometimes bravely opposing the eccentricities of power, cannot become an exceptional hero since he does not recognize the inhuman nature of colonization itself, and personally is unable to break with his childhood friend. So he only protests against

---

[6] A reference to one of the most destructive legacies of the Ceauşescu regime, which was the building up of a complex system of informers, blackmailing, threatening, beating and bribing people into informing on their nearest and dearest. Details of who informed on whom keep coming to light decades after the dictator's death, despoiling relationships for generations. The differences between those who volunteered to become informers and those who were tortured into signing documents over time have become blurred and thus many who suffered for their (partial or total resistance) are now besmirched forever.

Alexander's self-deification and the Greeks' excessive violence, which is exactly what makes him a modern hero: being full of doubts, making efforts to preserve his moral integrity yet remaining too hesitant, fallible, in short, dependent. His tragic flaw is his surviving attachment to his one-time friend when that friend has long-ago betrayed their common youthful ideals, and through that attachment being an accomplice in the communal oppression. He continues living in illusion about the possibility of compromise, of being simultaneously inside and outside, of practicing a kind of humanized colonization. Parmenion's fate becomes an example of how total power destroys not only enemies and rebels but the best features in those who basically support that power but try to stick to more human and humane values. His counterpoint, Betis, the leader of the last defenders of the Persian castle, represents uncompromising identity and choice. Betis is ready to sacrifice himself and his beloved rather than accept humiliating colonization, and has no time for doubts and hesitancies. While his heroic resistance deserves respect, his desperate black-and-white division of the world into allies and enemies, his hiding his feelings out of necessity, sounds cruel and inhuman. His fossilization demonstrates how such historical situations inevitably restrict even the best human values and, at the same time, it also calls attention to the danger of how naïve pondering, weighing choices and chances, such as Parmenion does, inevitably leads to masking the core situation and to relativizing the differences between the alien aggressors and the enslaved natives.

Symptomatic of his madness of self-deification, Alexander dictates the future into a chronicle as if it has already happened; so in his insanity of uncontrolled power Ceauşescu also had his history rewritten in schoolbooks and history books according to his megalomaniac desires and demanded that the descriptions of the present reflect his over-weaning fantasy. In the formation of the figures of the various Greeks and Persians in Sütő's play, the differences between the plight of the ruling nation and the defeated ethnic people become starkly outlined. It is true that the Greeks also suffer from despotism with their democratic values deeply endangered and even their individual rights (for instance, to choose one's wife) are lost, just as are the Persians'. But the latter—the conquered—in addition to their subjugation, as would be true of any subject under a dictatorial system, are also forced to give up their cultural values, their religion, their culture, their language and accept those of the rulers. The colonizers—as is well-known in postcolonial theories—feminize the colonized, that is, treat all the colonized as male chauvinists treat women (as second-rate citizens); hence women suffer a triple oppression. The misogynist Alexander's and Greek Governors' behavior and words abundantly demonstrate this as in, for example, the lust-infected strip-search of Eanna. Thales's prayer—that the Persians must learn and repeat—clearly brings together women and "barbarians:" "The gods be praised that by Their Grace / I was not born a wild beast / Neither a beast, nor a woman, / But a warrior: a man. / The gods be praised that by Their Grace / I was not born a barbarian ..."

Many of Sütő's main considerations in *The Suza Wedding Feast* had already appeared some ten years earlier in an essay entitled *The Persians* (later published together with the play in 1981), with the huge difference that in the essay the future still looks more promising than the present: on the day of Alexander's death the children born out of forced marriages began to "twitter in the language of their mothers, like the tiny birds of the fable, which once ate up the lion." No such light shines up from the play since by 1980 the playwright was unable to see any optimistic ending, only hopelessness and despair. Yet, as one of the distressed Persians says in *The Suza Wedding Feast*: "All the more reason ... to name the trouble, if you can't give voice to consolation. That also gives strength." With the examples of resistance in deep hopelessness, of a few characters' unbroken backbones (even when confronting torture) and of at least one example— that of Eanna—of a person able to unite moral steadfastness with human understanding, Sütő did give strength to the Hungarian minority in Romania during the darkest days of Ceauşescu's communist regime.

Csilla Bertha and Donald E. Morse

the suza wedding feast

cast of characters

PARMENION
EANNA
KLEITOS
DEMETRIOS
LUSIMAKHOS
KALLISTHENES
BETIS
BESSOS
YOUNG BESSOS
SUZIA
PHILIPPOS
ROXANNE
CAPTAIN OF THE GUARDS
Generals, Egyptian priests, soldiers, satraps,
Guards, Persian girls and women, children,
musicians
The Voice of Alexander the Great

act one

Scene: the Suza palace during the Changing of the guards. Trumpet fanfare sounds. GUARDS march entering and exiting. Before the GUARDS take their places in front of the throne room and the entrances, KLEITOS storms in and surveys the scene.

KLEITOS: Password?

CAPTAIN OF THE GUARDS: I beg to report to Lord Governor Kleitos: from Pella to India!

KLEITOS: And if our great leader, Alexander, appears?

CAPTAIN OF THE GUARDS: Glory to Alexander, may the Hellenic Empire live fevor!

KLEITOS: "Fevor!" You Persian wild ass! You're still swallowing the Greek word. You like our language so much that you'd eat it, wouldn't you?

CAPTAIN OF THE GUARDS: I have eaten mutton, I beg to report to you!

KLEITOS: Where did you serve before?

CAPTAIN OF THE GUARDS: Here, at the same place, I beg to report. Only . . .

KLEITOS: "Only" what?

CAPTAIN OF THE GUARDS: Under our King Darius.

KLEITOS: And have you woken up yet? Do you know where you are?

CAPTAIN OF THE GUARDS: I am at the same place, at Suza, I beg to report, only . . .

KLEITOS: "Only?"

CAPTAIN OF THE GUARDS: Glory to Alexander, may the Hellenic Empire live fevor.

KLEITOS: Forever! By your mother's camel udder! When everything is finished here you'll go to prison for two days and practice the word, "forever." I hope the others know it better than you.

GUARDS: Glory to Alexander, may the Hellenic Empire live forever!

KLEITOS: Our lord is feeling unwell today, so I want the greeting given less loudly.

GUARDS: Glory to Alexander, may the Hellenic Empire live forever!

KLEITOS: For today only, one person will give the greeting. Not you. The other one.

A GUARD: Glory . . .

KLEITOS: Forever. To prayer.

GUARDS: The gods be praised . . .

KLEITOS: Whose prayer are you saying?

CAPTAIN OF THE GUARDS: One that is now ours, I beg to report.

KLEITOS: But who said it first? You dumb beasts. Thales. And who was Thales? You'll learn a little Greek history as well. To prayer.

GUARDS:

The gods be praised that by Their Grace
    I was not born a wild beast.

3

Neither a beast, nor a woman,
But a warrior: a man.

The gods be praised that by Their Grace
I was not born a puling female
Not a chameleon-like woman
But a hero and a man.

The gods be praised that by Their Grace
I was not born a barbarian,
Not a Persian, no alien
But a great, immortal Greek!
Hurrah!

KLEITOS: Hurrah! And as for your brains, keep them in good shape because we're in for a difficult day and a difficult night, but all the more glorious and significant for that.

FIRST GUARD: Free plunder again.

KLEITOS: Alexander forbade free plunder. From today on, in all Persian territory, that is, in Greek Macedonian land, and especially here in the town of Suza, there will be peace and brotherhood. Brotherization. Otherwise as for looting, I hope you have no reason to complain. Let me know if you have.

SECOND GUARD: In Persepholis we got seven days for looting and for dealing with women.

KLEITOS: That was before brotherization had been declared. Chisel our Lord's idea into your brains: it's not that we like the Persians the less, but the union with them the more. Do you also understand—You, "Forever?"

CAPTAIN OF THE GUARDS: Yes, Sir! The Persians the less, the union the more.

KLEITOS: That, too, in prison—in solitary confinement. And you, you complaining burglar's kisser, what's wrong with looting? I can see that you haven't been sitting idle in Suza either. Jewelry?

SECOND SOLDIER: For one wife of mine and three girls, I beg to report.

KLEITOS: Velvet, brocade, and such?

SECOND SOLDIER: Six bags, I beg to report.

KLEITOS: Broads?

SECOND SOLDIER: Only three, I beg to report.

KLEITOS: So you're saving some for later as well. And you?

THIRD SOLDIER: Thirteen maidens, I beg to report.

KLEITOS: No jewelry?

FIRST SOLDIER: Thurasbulos is only after virgins I beg to report.

KLEITOS: And they don't wear jewelry?

THIRD SOLDIER: The ones wearing jewels are already defective, I beg to report.

KLEITOS: Where are they defective?

THIRD SOLDIER: Down there, I beg to report.

KLEITOS: That's just natural. You always get women, like money, from someone else's hands, my son. Not directly from the mint.

THIRD SOLDIER: Yes, Sir! In the case of women, honesty and jewelry are a matter of exchange, I beg to report.

KLEITOS: Are you Epicurean?

THIRD SOLDIER: Thurasbulos, I beg to report.

KLEITOS: And you, sheep's disaster, how many virgins?

FOURTH SOLDIER: None, I beg to report.

KLEITOS: Are you only after ladies of the evening?

FOURTH SOLDIER: I don't care about women, I beg to report.

KLEITOS: Do you live in fear of your wife? She's a long way off.

THIRD SOLDIER: That one doesn't fear, I beg to report.

KLEITOS: Then what does he do?

CAPTAIN OF THE GUARDS: He's deballed, I beg to report. (*All the GUARDS guffaw.*)

KLEITOS: Deballed. You're the one, whose wife had you castrated so you couldn't deceive her?

(More guffawing.)

FOURTH SOLDIER: It happened by order of Alexander for sexual violence in a prohibited time, I beg to report.

KLEITOS: That's different. What's the moral of it? All of you, who aren't yet castrated or aren't shortened by an obstinate head, remember: Alexander knows why and what he does. Is that clear?

GUARDS: We beg to report to Lord Governor: clear.

KLEITOS: Clear, but let it be clear in a lower voice, I've warned you. So: we'll have a luminescent night. The most famous hymenal night of the human race—of course, going together with a wedding feast. Alexander today is going to marry the most exquisite woman, Roxanne, the

6

wife of his heroic enemy, Darius. Before this happy event our Lord will be sanctified as a god by the chief priests of Amon. Our leader, Alexander will become the earthly son of Zeus-Amon and from that moment on it'll be forbidden to look up at him when addressing him. The proper form of tribute to a god is the bowed head. Is that clear? Quietly. (*The GUARDS express their respect with bowed heads.*) Darius himself will also participate in the wedding feast so that he may know the special joy of the defeated. Because he who lays down his weapons gives his wife, his daughter, his soul, his gods to the victors. In exchange he receives our gods, the real ones, and the right to speak our language and to observe our ancient customs. It's the generosity of Alexander that—under those conditions—we're ready to absorb anyone whether he be Persian, Scythian, Hindu, Massageta, Egyptian, Maccabean, or any other barbarian. What's more: they can even use our names. Let them possess them; the Grecian name will shape its wearer to resemble itself anyway, let's hope, within a short time. What's your name, you, for example, you "forever?"

CAPTAIN OF THE GUARDS: Ali, I beg to report.

KLEITOS: Ali. You couldn't afford a longer name, you're so poor. Alibulos . . . doesn't that sound better? Especially in the case of a Captain of the Guards. You're in a trustworthy position. Well?

CAPTAIN OF THE GUARDS: According to the belief of our ancestors, I beg to report, he who exchanges his name, exchanges his soul, I beg to report.

KLEITOS: Soul. So you've a soul with which to think about what I've just said. Back to Darius! When his head men, the satraps, lead him to Alexander you should have an eagle's eyes, jackal's nose, and tiger's ears. The king is good-willed, but his chief, Betis, who, as you know, has not yet surrendered, may smuggle assassins into the palace among the king's men. The bodyguards inside are also on the alert, but you know where any mistake you make will lead you: up onto the cross. Is that clear? The cross is clear. (*Cheering from the palace square: "Glory to Alexander!"*) Do you hear that? Among the crowd there's a great number of Persians and all sorts of barbarians. Including some would-be assassins. Maybe they cheer the loudest. So whoever does not know the password and tries to enter here must be taken to prison and to the star chamber for interrogation. Is that clear?

CAPTAIN OF THE GUARDS: Prison and star chamber.

KLEITOS: Because they garland their sentences with flowers, and wrap their knives in silk. Alexander must respond with gladness if the defeated are enthusiastic about him, but you must not trust this street theatre-faithfulness. Your task is to be suspicious every minute. And now listen.

ALEXANDER'S VOICE (*from the window of the throne room*): My faithful Persians, my brethren! I'm happy. You've put down your weapons, and you're going to take them up again on my side. The war itself wasn't our goal; it was only the means to wake up the East. Asia Minor, Phoenicia, and Egypt have surrendered.

8

Phrygia, Lydia, Tarsus, Hellicarnasus, Suza, and Persepholis are defeated. Darius is in hiding, but we expect his surrender. His mother, his wife, and his children fled to me, and not a hair on their heads will be harmed. Persia does not exist any more in its old form, but it'll become a strong arm of the united empire. Let us stretch our brotherly hands out to one another and, if anybody objects to the great wedding feast that begins today, you shall declare him our common enemy. Because it's not that we like the Persians the less, but the union with them, even in blood, the more. From tonight Roxanne, the ex-queen is your future queen but at my side. I would like my General Staff and my whole army to follow my example as soon as possible. Don't be averse to us, and you'll be happy in the Hellenic Empire!

(The crowd cheers. PARMENION arrives upset.)

KLEITOS: Parmenion! What's happening over there? Disperse!

(The GUARDS exit.)

PARMENION: Our leader's latest ruse. I couldn't dissuade him from it. He's orating in Persian costume—to our enemies. And he's going to marry that poison-monger Roxanne—he's gone mad.

KLEITOS: You can say that. You're his friend. Patroklos and Achilleus! You, together with Kallisthenes, are also privy to his secrets. But that he's gone mad: I'm not allowed to believe that. I haven't heard it, and Demetrios, especially, mustn't hear it. And if I were you I wouldn't express an opinion on Roxanne—neither good nor bad.

PARMENION: You'll choke on swallowed opinions. If you don't choke, they'll sit heavy on your stomach and other organs. Look around and see who looks ill. Kallisthenes, for example. He's withering from swallowed opinions.

KLEITOS: You're more upset today than ever.

PARMENION: If I were a doctor, I wouldn't ask the patient what he'd eaten, but what he'd been forced to silence, swallow, digest, and not vomit up . . .

KLEITOS: What happened to you?

PARMENION: We drank wine, threw dice. I gave my opinion about Roxanne, then he said we should wrestle, he was very cheerful, but suddenly his face became distorted, and he began to strangle me. I've never seen that murderous impulse in his eyes before. I had to yell at him to bring him back to himself.

KLEITOS: I've heard about that. And then?

PARMENION: It was as if he'd been awakened from a nightmare; he looked at me as if I were someone he didn't recognize and he said without shouting—as he usually speaks nowadays—but whispering and terribly sad that he didn't want to see me any more.

KLEITOS: He said the same thing other times, too. Don't take it so to heart.

PARMENION: But I can't forget his whispered sadness. He was desperate, Kleitos, like someone who'd fallen into a final loneliness. He's totally alone . . . I can't help him any longer.

KLEITOS: You want to help him, but you only upset him, especially with what you say about Roxanne. Friendship can be strong, but bedfellowship is even stronger.

PARMENION: And what if she poisons him?

KLEITOS: It's not in her interest. Women aren't patriots. Their battlefield is the bed.

PARMENION: I can't get over it: he puts on Persian clothes, Egyptian priests sanctify him as a god, he sinks down to the level of Eastern thinking. All of Athens will laugh at him.

KLEITOS: Or praise him. Like the Persians.

PARMENION: The Persians are smarter than that. They proclaim their loyalty in order to survive their defeat. The delegations are arriving. Their foreheads are scraping the floor, their humility hides their faces, and thereby their intentions. You'd better send observers among the crowds.

KLEITOS: Anyone who doesn't cheer the new order will be watched.

PARMENION: And that goes double for anyone who cheers it the loudest, if he's a Persian. I prefer Betis.

KLEITOS: That mad resister?

PARMENION: He doesn't reveal any intention, except the one he actually has. At least he's a man.

KLEITOS: Guards!

CAPTAIN OF THE GUARDS (*comes in running*): At your command!

KLEITOS: Double the Guards at the entrance to the palace! Send civilian observers out into the middle of the cheering crowds!

CAPTAIN OF THE GUARDS: Yes, Sir! (*Exits, then returns.*) Where do I get the civilians from? I beg to report.

KLEITOS: The same place you got them from before, you dumb ox. From among the soldiers.

CAPTAIN OF THE GUARDS: Yes, Sir! (*Exits.*)

(*PHILIPPOS enters.*)

PARMENION: The other poison-monger. Halt, you bastard son of Asklepios!

PHILIPPOS: Our Lord has a fever. I must give him some medicine.

PARMENION: And what's Roxanne doing?

PHILIPPOS: She's preparing for her wedding and she's having her maids' hair combed. They're guessing whose wives they're going to be. (*Tries to exit.*)

PARMENION: Philippos, show me that medicine.

PHILIPPOS: It's the same as yesterday . . .

PARMENION: Show it to me!

KLEITOS: Show it to him if he asks you to.

PHILIPPOS: Please, Parmenion, stop being so suspicious. It hurts me personally. Borrow some trust in me from Alexander.

PARMENION: Did Roxanne send the medicine?

PHILIPPOS: It's said to be better than my concoctions. Yesterday you also suspected that it was poison, and yet Alexander took it laughing in your face. And he's alive and getting better. Isn't that enough for you?

PARMENION: It is not. Let me see it.

PHILIPPOS: Even the air can contaminate it. I'm not going to show it to you.

PARMENION: It's sent by Roxanne, so you're not going to show it to me. Guards!

(Three guards run in.)

KLEITOS: Philippos, don't be obstinate. He's having a bad day today . . .

PARMENION: Here with that bag of poison!

PHILIPPOS: Don't touch it. A cholera epidemic rages. If you touch it I can't be held responsible. And anyway I'll report this suspicion to Alexander . . .

PARMENION: Here with it or I'll have you stripped!

PHILIPPOS: All right, you can see it, but I won't give it to our Lord. And the responsibility is yours. . . . I've been serving for ten years . . . shame and scandal . . . Here you are!

PARMENION: You say this is a fever killer.

PHILIPPOS: And a pain killer.

PARMENION: And how much do you want him to take?

PHILIPPOS: Two little spoonfuls.

PARMENION: Let's see what opinion these two little spoonfuls give about your honesty and about that of your lady Roxanne.

KLEITOS: You're mad! There are dogs around here who . . .

PARMENION: Woe to Alexander if his friends are replaced by dogs. Especially by that bitch.

(PARMENION takes the medicine. Silence. KLEITOS sends the guards away without a word.)

PHILIPPOS: But I've told you . . .

PARMENION: Don't speak yet. (*Waiting.*) But of course you're all such cowards that you would never give him fast-acting poison. Well, this time you appear to have escaped, Philippos.

PHILIPPOS: A pure conscience doesn't escape. (*Exits.*)

KLEITOS: Roxanne's poison-makers are better than ours. You shouldn't have let Philippos go. So that you should see, while dying, how I'd throw his heart and liver to the dogs.

PARMENION: Thank you. It's not poison.

KLEITOS: And what if it is?

PARMENION: Then I die before him. (*Ironically.*) Out of pure good manners.

KLEITOS: I don't understand this capricious friendship . . . relationship . . . nearly love . . .

PARMENION: A love that has begun to spoil.

KLEITOS: But is it only because of Roxanne and his status as a god? (*Cunningly.*) There must be something more to it.

PARMENION: Yes, of course there is: brain damage.

KLEITOS: ?

PARMENION: Concerning all of us . . .

KLEITOS: All of us—me, too—brain damage? What are you talking about?

PARMENION: You're also part of it.

KLEITOS: But, what are you talking about?

PARMENION: I feel dizzy.

KLEITOS: You feel dizzy. Are you sick? The poison.

PARMENION: The poison.

KLEITOS: Tell me, Parmenion. That brain damage . . .

PARMENION: You're inquiring too late. My eyes are blurring.

KLEITOS: Do you see colorful flocks of butterflies? Maroon clouds of butterflies?

PARMENION: How do you know?

KLEITOS: That's what the Persians prepare. That kind of poison. So that passing away will be pleasant. Tell me, what does he want with me?

PARMENION: With you. And with me? Of course you don't care.

KLEITOS: I care about your fate, also, but you know it yourself. Tell me mine, don't keep it a secret. No point in keeping secrets any longer.

PARMENION: Any longer? Why wouldn't there be?

KLEITOS: Because you're a stupid dumbbell who exaggerates faithfulness.

PARMENION: Exaggerates . . .

KLEITOS: Up to the point of suicide. And what for? So that he should kick you out? So that you could be a toy for his caprice. But all of us are that. Me, too.

PARMENION: You, too.

KLEITOS: You shouldn't have taken the poison. Oh, you suicidal Parmenion. Tell me something about his plans concerning me . . .

PARMENION: Wonderful . . .

KLEITOS: Wonderful?

PARMENION: What he's done. He's awakened a sleeping giant. We wanted to civilize all the East, and now he's running to his destruction in front of my eyes.

KLEITOS: You'd better worry about yourself. And tell me, what does he want with me?

PARMENION: We started together from Pella . . . from our birthplace. . . . In ten years we've reached India. Do you know why he succeeded?

KLEITOS: Because he's brave and invincible, I know it very well. That's not what I want you to talk about. Look here! You're gazing into nothing. Do you see the clouds of butterflies?

PARMENION: I do. Maroon flocks of butterflies . . .

KLEITOS: I can't help you. Philippos! I wish he were here already. But in the meantime tell me . . . what you know about me, . . . About our uncertain situation. One day you're a governor, the next day a dog groomer. . . . Won't you give away anything . . . before you die?

PARMENION: Oh how much you worry about me! Oh my dear friend, you hope for a secret from out of my death. . . . Fly, fly, colorful butterflies. . . . The Persian poison-makers are inventive murderers . . . passing away is really beautiful this way . . .

KLEITOS: Don't die, Parmenion. Don't die. Talk.

PARMENION: Alexander was never wrong because he had respect in him. The respect for facts.

KLEITOS: Oh, you're raving again.

PARMENION: I'm saying it so you'll know. When I die you should tell him the same. That respect for facts. . . . Not for the gods in heaven, not for Zeus, Apollo, not the oracles of Delphi, Dodonna—that he mentioned only for the sake of the crowd—but for Gods of Facts. This enormous diversity of people in the East, this Babel has been his God of Facts up to this moment . . .

KLEITOS: I know, I know, I know, but that isn't what I'm interested in.

PARMENION: He himself made up what the gods should suggest, order, prophesy to him. He's been the god and his own subject in the same person. But now . . .

KLEITOS: Shove your philosophy! Tell me: do I remain the governor? And Demetrios. You know . . . or don't know . . . he hates you.

PARMENION: As if Anthaeus, his sense of reality, has escaped him.

(Egyptian Priests parade.)

KLEITOS: Amon's priests . . .

PARMENION: These are the ones who made him drunk.

KLEITOS: How much time do you think you've left? How can I help you?

PARMENION: What a great man he's been and what a tiny god he'll make having been dulled by the golden smoke of these desert jackals . . .

KLEITOS: Don't slander him. I'll tell him everything. If you don't confess to me. . . . About me. I beg you, something about me . . .

17

PARMENION: We need our leader as the most powerful being on earth, because if he were already a god, he'd have to be in the sky, and we'd be left without him. And the only thing I'm afraid of is that we'll be left without him. Do you know, Kleitos, what being a god means?

KLEITOS: Another elevation.

PARMENION: A blind alley.

KLEITOS (*frightened*): You're saying awful things. Because you know you're going to die. But die usefully and tell me why he trusts Demetrios more than me. That rat who slandered me. He slandered you, too. I fear that . . .

PARMENION: In me the poison—in you the fear. Oh you, the bravest of the brave, the hero of all fears, you inverted Achilleus.

KLEITOS: In the battle of Gaugamela. . .

PARMENION: You behaved differently. Well, is it worth winning, Kleitos? If victory makes one so rotten?

KLEITOS: You're raving. How many times have I asked you: what's going to happen to me? Me, Governor Kleitos! Don't you understand: me!

PARMENION: Me, me, me, to me! What a desert-world of selfishness. Everything else is triviality, is nothing. What's going to happen to me, Governor Kleitos. Not to Alexander, not to the Empire, not to the great aims: to me, Kleitos . . . Demetrios . . . Lusimakhos. So this is the foundation of the Empire.

KLEITOS: Stop mocking! The dying shouldn't mock. You yourself, aren't you selfish? Don't you cling desperately to his friendship?

PARMENION: I worry and wish to save him from making mistakes . . . water . . . a little water . . .

(*EANNA enters.*)

KLEITOS: Hey, you, young lady! Water here, quickly. Quickly! I should run for Philippos, but he's with our Lord, so I can't disturb him.

(*EANNA brings water.*)

EANNA: Here you are, sir. (*She makes PARMENION drink.*)

KLEITOS: Don't die, Parmenion.

PARMENION: Who are you?

EANNA: EANNA, sir.

KLEITOS: Excuse me for shouting. You must understand me.

PARMENION: What did you give me to drink?

EANNA: Water, sir. Pure water.

PARMENION (*looks long at EANNA*): Pure water. The water of life. I'm already better for it.

EANNA: I wish you recovery, sir. (*Exits.*)

KLEITOS: And you must know . . .

PARMENION: Who's this young woman?

KLEITOS: My friendship isn't like that of Demetrios. Because he hates you, he'd like to take your place beside Alexander—to become his confidential friend.

PARMENION: I know. That woman, I think I've seen her before.

KLEITOS: But I—as you very well know—highly appreciate you.

PARMENION: You highly appreciate—my secrets. Higher than my life.

KLEITOS: You're wrong, I worry about your life. And I really thought that you would die before my eyes.

PARMENION: You didn't think, but you hoped.

KLEITOS: You slander me. And are you any better?

PARMENION: I was just acting a part.

KLEITOS: Why did you do that?

PARMENION: Because in my friend, Kleitos—I thought I recognized the grave robber. It's not worth even dying, Kleitos. The living, seeing the dead, worry about themselves.

KLEITOS: Excuse me if you misunderstood something.

PARMENION: I understood that according to you in my faithfulness I'm a stupid jerk.

KLEITOS: Watch out, that's not what I said. Faithfulness exaggerated. . . . That's what I said. But "blind alley" was your line. Being a god is a blind alley. Such audacity can be said only by someone who's dying.

PARMENION: That's what misled you. Only those who are dying tell the truth.

KLEITOS: A mean game, Parmenion, although I admit you're playing with your life. He sent you away from his presence so you're playing with your life.

PARMENION: Because without him my life is worthless, but now I'm the sadder for my experience.

KLEITOS: He doesn't want to see you any more.

PARMENION: Around him faithfulness is cautious, and selfishness grows all the greater: "What's going to happen to me, to me!"

KLEITOS (*frightened*): I did not proclaim cautious faithfulness! I considered your poison test an exaggeration—stupidity. How do you know it wasn't poison? Slowly killing poison. Lest this game of yours not turn serious tomorrow. The game of death that this beautiful young woman can't ease . . .

(PHILIPPOS enters.)

PARMENION: It'll be all the easier. I've had the rehearsal.

PHILIPPOS: Our Lord took the medicine and feels better. I told him about your poison test, and rejoice: he burst into tears. He wants to see you urgently. Next time you shouldn't doubt me.

PARMENION: Next time I'll search you better. You've got a lot of pockets and Roxanne has slow killing poison, too.

PHILIPPOS: Then watch yourself. And tell me if you see red clouds of butterflies . . .

ALEXANDER'S VOICE: Parmenion! Where are you Parmenion?

PARMENION (*happily*): Here I am, Alexander. I'm coming, Alexander!

KLEITOS: Be careful what you say about me. The blind alley was your line.

ALEXANDER'S VOICE: Parmenion, my only friend!

PARMENION: Yes, I said it. And I also know: you mustn't say anything to your friend that you wouldn't say straight to the face of the god.

21

(*Quickly exits.*)

(*DEMETRIOS enters.*)

KLEITOS: Have you heard, Demetrios? He's raving.

DEMETRIOS: I know from our Lord that he took a poison test. You see, that's how to do it. Not the words of faithfulness, but the deeds of faithfulness . . .

KLEITOS: And if he dies soon?

DEMETRIOS: He won't die. The concoction was sent by Roxanne and therefore it must be an aphrodisiac. You know very well that there'll be the great hymenal night. My friend, you don't know women, they won't be so foolish as to shorten their lives by a phallus. Especially by that of Alexander. . . . And what else did he say?

KLEITOS: That Alexander's being a god is a blind alley.

DEMETRIOS: Ah ha. That's interesting, but he's bold enough to say the same to the face of our Lord and then that statement of his has no significance for us.

KLEITOS: Is his chief defense—his directness?

DEMETRIOS: Probably, but don't try to imitate him. You weren't a childhood playmate of our Lord.

KLEITOS: And I'm not his drinking buddy today. Demetrios, tell me the secret plan from which you left me out again although we're on the same level as governors.

DEMETRIOS: Next time I'll be left out of something and you'll be the one initiated. The dice and trust pass in turn from one to another.

KLEITOS: Then what shall I prepare for?

DEMETRIOS: For a test of faithfulness.

KLEITOS: Will we have to fight? To die under the castle of Betis?

DEMETRIOS: The Persians are coming. But not with a regular army. Exciting details from Kallisthenes—what a chronicle!

KLEITOS: Demetrios, now you also use circumlocution.

DEMETRIOS: It's always the one who comes last from Alexander who uses circumlocution and who's also the smartest. So what's important is not that one should be the first to enter, but to be the last to exit from him.

KLEITOS: All your words are blurred. At such times my stomach trembles. Test of faithfulness. Didn't we face death a hundred times? Do we always have to top all previous tests of faithfulness?

DEMETRIOS: Don't be furious, don't be scared. A pleasant test of faithfulness. For now only this much: at the third trumpet fanfare open the main entrance to the eastern wing of the palace.

KLEITOS: Roxanne?

DEMETRIOS: In person. Darius's honest wife, ex-wife, and her entourage, ladies, followers, satraps. And with that a new kind of war commences.

(Persian women, among them, EANNA, SUZIA, Ariane, Persephone, and so on, walk towards the throne room. After them come the Master of Ceremonies and KALLISTHENES with his large locked book.)

KLEITOS: War?!

DEMETRIOS: Look, here march by the battlefields. A honey-sweet battlefield of hills and clusters of grapes.

KLEITOS: Where are you taking them, Kallisthenes?

KALLISTHENES: To an inspection. But don't ask me anything else. I can't answer.

DEMETRIOS: We'll keep the last two for a little while. Reasons of security. . . . Come here, you beautiful pomegranate. What's your name?

SUZIA (*cheerfully*): I'm Suzia, sir, the daughter of Bessos.

DEMETRIOS: And how do you like it here in the royal court?

SUZIA: Now, I feel fine, sir. My people are alive and are coming here to the wedding.

DEMETRIOS: Would you like to be married, too?

SUZIA: Oh, I'm too young for that, sir.

DEMETRIOS: But you're big enough not to fall out of bed.

SUZIA: If I grab hold hard enough . . .

DEMETRIOS: Do the handsome warriors court you?

SUZIA: Oh yes, often . . .

DEMETRIOS: And do you like them?

SUZIA: I haven't chosen yet, sir. Because I'm too young.

DEMETRIOS: But if you grab hold hard enough. . . . You'll become a little bigger. And what do you tell your admirers?

SUZIA: Well, I say:

Sensuous shepherd, I'm crying out to you,

This way, my shepherd, step into the house of
love,
Be glad and cheerful, my beloved other half.
Desire is golden, love is diamond.

DEMETRIOS: Diamond. . . . Now look at this little
chicken. What'll you know when you grow
feathers? Let's see the other one. You're
gloomy like poison in the bag. . . . That one
remains here, Kallisthenes. Take the little one,
she's not dangerous.

KALLISTHENES: I can leave her behind, but you'll
be accountable for her.

DEMETRIOS: Don't worry—just go ahead.

(KALLISTHENES leaves with the Young Women.)

DEMETRIOS: What's your name?

EANNA: Eanna.

DEMETRIOS: Whose bedfellow are you?

EANNA: Nobody's, sir.

DEMETRIOS: My poor bird. How is it possible?

EANNA: By the grace of God. And a little bit of help
from me.

DEMETRIOS: That's right! If a girl is protected, she
will protect herself. The two-faced god of
virginity. And whom do you expect for yourself
tonight?

EANNA: Nobody, sir.

DEMETRIOS: But the two-faced god is overthrown.
Not only Roxanne but also her ladies-in-
waiting go into the arms of Hymen . . .

EANNA: Who must come will come.

DEMETRIOS: And what must come, you beautiful

pomegranate. You don't speak our language well yet, but it doesn't matter. In love it's limbs that talk, isn't that right, Kleitos? What's more, the lack of words is an advantage. They don't disturb what's most important, what has to happen without exchanging ideas.

EANNA: What do you want to do with me?

DEMETRIOS: We cannot strip-search everyone. We only take random samples. Show us your leg.

EANNA: It's not yours, sir.

KLEITOS: This one hasn't seen a cock yet. Her crown is intact.

DEMETRIOS: Show us your bosom.

EANNA: It's not yours, sir.

DEMETRIOS: Let's see your diamond navel.

EANNA: It's not yours, sir.

DEMETRIOS: Not yours, not yours! You use the negative in our language without a mistake, but the first thing you have to learn is yes. Yes, yes . . .

KLEITOS: Haven't you got a vial of poison under your clothes?

EANNA: No! Sir, don't molest me.

DEMETRIOS: Little pomegranate, I'm not molesting you. Show us your leg!

EANNA: I'll report you to Alexander.

KLEITOS: Let her go.

DEMETRIOS: Don't put words in her mouth. And you, don't threaten me because I order you for the sake of our Lord's security: show us your bosom.

KLEITOS: You may have a dagger . . . or poison . . . show us your leg, your bosom, your diamond navel.

EANNA: No! No! No! (*She bites him.*)

KLEITOS: Oh you wild beast! Not even Cerberus had sharper teeth!

EANNA: Alexander forbade freedom plunder. Help!

KLEITOS: Go to hell!

DEMETRIOS: Go nowhere! Guards!

(CAPTAIN OF THE GUARDS enters with one of his men.)

DEMETRIOS: Suspected assassin! A thorough search!

KLEITOS: But not you, let whatshisname do it. The castrated one. With him no reports of violence have any credibility.

CAPTAIN OF THE GUARDS: Thurasbulos!

(FOURTH SOLDIER enters running, the other soldier returns to his place.)

KLEITOS (*to the CAPTAIN OF THE GUARDS*): And since you're Persian, you're impartial—in this case.

DEMETRIOS: Search her!

(The Two Soldiers pounce on her.)

EANNA: Infamous slander! Lies! I'm no assassin. Help! I've no dagger, poison, or anything else on me! I'm Roxanne's lady. You killed my father, but I'm no assassin! I'm your enemy, but I've no evil intentions. Help!

DEMETRIOS: Shut her up!

KLEITOS: She'll alarm the whole palace . . .

EANNA: Leave me alone! Take pity on me! You also have sisters, younger sisters and mothers!

DEMETRIOS: But above and before them is the order.

KLEITOS: Send her to hell!

EANNA: Freedom plunder is forbidden!

DEMETRIOS: Shut her up! Search all her clothing, her every little joint!

(The Soldiers tie her up, and put a rag in her mouth.)

KLEITOS: Let's hope she's not the queen's favorite!

DEMETRIOS (*blinded by rage and lust because of the girl*): The Guards are witnesses: this is neither robbery nor violence. She was on her way there, so we search her and thereby do our duty. Alexander's father was assassinated by such people! What if in the meantime her legs and boson become exposed to daylight. Well-hidden daggers must be looked for in well-hidden places. Put everything in my hands!

(The GUARDS rip off EANNA's clothes piece by piece and throw them to DEMETRIOS who in turn throws them to KLEITOS.)

DEMETRIOS: The veil floats nicely when you carry its wearer to bed.

KLEITOS: If your arms are not old.

DEMETRIOS: But it's possible to strangle someone with it—the enchanted lover most of all.

KLEITOS: You as well as me.

DEMETRIOS: Necklace, diadem, combs, hairpins, disorder in every embrace, let's see which is the murderous instrument intended for our Lord?

KLEITOS: And the poison—from the sweet hidden place.

DEMETRIOS: Our great king, Philippos, you should've been more alert, the knives jumped into your heart from women's hairdos and panties!

KLEITOS: Out of fine fabric. . . . Oh . . .

DEMETRIOS: We'll take better care of your son, Alexander—We'll nicely peel the Persian fruits brought to his bed.

KLEITOS: The pomegranate is lovely without its peel.

DEMETRIOS: As for me, Kleitos, I'd even taste it, but unfortunately it's forbidden where it's the sweetest.

KLEITOS: We don't know how the order reads!

DEMETRIOS: Hey you, sleepyheads, get a move on with that search, and get further inside, downward, in the shadowy places. Wind-stirring skirt, velvet and brocade, Eanna, you're the daughter of a great lord!—don't worry about the underwear—the less that covers a woman the more valuable she is! Hurry up!

KLEITOS: Hurry up!

DEMETRIOS: Kleitos, fragrance of rose oil!

KLEITOS: So there must be a rosebush, too.

DEMETRIOS: You're right, but before that--there higher up those two young kids, you jerks! Tenderly part them, it has happened that a

29

knife dropped out between them in the marriage bed. But even from lower down, from the roots of the thighs, Kleitos! Now pay attention and don't drool, but let your brain work and understand our Lord's wisdom.

KLEITOS: Let's leave her to get dressed.

DEMETRIOS: Wait! Do you think we've triumphed? Provinces and towns lie before our feet. But not under us!

KLEITOS: The search should be called . . .

DEMETRIOS: Wait! Suza, the treasure of Persepolis is nothing, it's only the surface! The colonized, the satraps will arrive and will bring expensive gifts: triviality! They'll shout: Long Live Alexander! Lie! They'll pay taxes, and they'll like us better than we like ourselves and our traditional weaknesses. They'll out-Hellenize us and yet our victory is still in doubt.

KLEITOS: In doubt?

DEMETRIOS: If we don't tame their women. That is a long term project.

KLEITOS: I swear you're very wise.

DEMETRIOS: The castle of Betis still stands, open and hidden resistance is flaming—but we won't sacrifice any more soldiers, any more blood, to take their only remaining castle.

KLEITOS: Why shouldn't we?

DEMETRIOS: We'll take it on the Mound of Venus of Persian women!

KLEITOS: So that is the new strategy! (*Pointing to the pieces of clothing*.) And what in heaven is this?

DEMETRIOS: The little heaven—what in heaven?

What stupidity in a smart man! Go and caress her, too. Be more daring! She's beautiful. Here, see the meaning of my words: After the surface we need the inside of Persia, Egypt, Syria.

KLEITOS: Of course.

DEMETRIOS: And, do you know where that inside is? Where this beautiful woman made her mistake in our language. She said instead of "free plunder," "freedom plunder." Where her blunders light the path pointing towards her own people. That's where we have to fight the new battles. Into Troy we smuggled a wooden horse; here, my friend, fertilizing phalluses. A good phallus makes the strongest phalanx. I've already composed a march on this subject, listen:

> A good phallus makes the best phalanx!
> Betis' castle still stands!
> Women in its loopholes
> Sweet apertures in the holes

Soldiers: Forward! And you two, also, back to your places!

(The Two Soldiers exit.)

KLEITOS: "Betis' castle still stands! Women in its loopholes." Let her go.

(DEMETRIOS removes the ropes from EANNA.)

DEMETRIOS: Forgive us, E-E-Eanna. Our interest was official although it might appear personal.

EANNA: Gods, I give you thanks . . .

31

KLEITOS: Your gods do deserve sacrifices. We didn't hurt you.

EANNA: "Betis' castle still stands . . ."

DEMETRIOS: Stands. Because we haven't attacked it for long . . .

EANNA: My dear father's castle. He's the only one who can hold it. You're defending it, my father. Thank you jackals, for the ignominy: in exchange for your good news. BETIS' castle still stands . . . our last refuge. . . . My father is alive, O Gods! O Gods, BETIS' castle still stands. My father, my dear father, Roxanne lied . . . Betis' castle still stands . . . O merciful Gods . . . (*She weeps.*)

ALEXANDER'S VOICE: In the name of universal order, of the all-reconciling Spirit, I ask and command all of you to . . . (*Trumpets sound. LUSIMAKHOS enters.*)

KLEITOS (*frightened*): Lusimakhos!

LUSIMAKHOS: What are you doing here? Why is that girl crying?

DEMETRIOS: She was on her way *there*, so we had to strip search her.

KLEITOS: She's Betis's daughter.

LUSIMAKHOS: Madmen!

DEMETRIOS: If anyone has to be searched, then the daughter of Betis certainly must be. For His sake.

LUSIMAKHOS: "For His sake?" when you have no idea about His latest plan. Daughter of Betis . . .

KLEITOS: I told you . . .

LUSIMAKHOS: My little fig flower, forgive me for their lack of manners. Your father is alive, and he'll make peace.

EANNA: My father?

LUSIMAKHOS: Your father, the chief. He'll make peace. Because we stretch out our right hand and offer peace.

EANNA: May he be cursed if he accepts it.

DEMETRIOS: Don't speak for him.

(The Master of Ceremonies enters with the Young Women seen earlier.)

LUSIMAKHOS: Master of Ceremonies! Dress up this one also. Put jewels on her. The Treasury won't begrudge it.

KLEITOS: Another new decision, and again made without me!

LUSIMAKHOS: He sends the message to you through me. You will hear it. Daughter of Betis, what's your name?

DEMETRIOS: Eanna.

LUSIMAKHOS: Eanna, cheer up. All will be well. Your father lives and will make peace.

EANNA: Never!

LUSIMAKHOS: Master of Ceremonies, take them away and get them dressed up. *(The Young Women exit, EANNA with them.)*

DEMETRIOS *(singing in a low voice)*: "A good phallus makes the best phalanx . . ." That's the limit of my information.

KLEITOS: I don't understand a thing.

LUSIMAKHOS: Because the brain of our Lord moves incessantly, and you with this strip search . . . "Phallus . . ." How could you talk about such things to the feminine gender? You should tell about the desire of the heart, you crude Hellenic goat! About the power and right of love above all. Above borders, languages, customs, and old fashioned morals. You should tell about Venus. . . . That won't frighten women. And then with Venus can come . . . whatever must.

DEMETRIOS: I've spoken of Venus.

KLEITOS: Her mound.

LUSIMAKHOS: But why her mound and not her essence?—that her power extends out to every mortal creature and it must be received with joy. Venus, my friend, who can command even the sea. With nice words. She travels on a shell and decorates every affection with pearls. You mustn't search, but evoke the Karis and the Horas—in the words of Pheita—through persuasion. You should mention the joys of Hymenios and not Phallos! Because women, although they like it, hate to hear about it. Because, first of all, they like to deceive themselves. They desire Hymenios, but it's better if, instead of the details of the body, you speak more poetically about singing birds and about the little golden cart that's pulled by Aphrodite's sparrows. Well, something along those lines rather than ripping their clothes off! Zeus took the wives of all his enemies but how, my friends? How did he fertilize the daughter of King Minos in the windowless tower? In the form of a shower of gold. The same way Zeus's son now . . .

DEMETRIOS: As for our purpose: we've already failed with the shower of gold.

LUSIMAKHOS: Soft words sometimes are as good as swords or even battering rams.

KLEITOS: Of course it's always the one who comes last from Alexander who's the smartest.

(Second trumpet sounds.)

LUSIMAKHOS: At the third we will receive Roxanne. In the meantime let's see how many we are: Kleitos, Demetrios, Lusimakhos, and Parmenion.

KLEITOS: If he's still alive.

LUSIMAKHOS: He is, and he'll be here. The General Staff. *(Shouts.)* Lord Generals!

A GUARD: Lord Generals!

(The Generals march in.)

KLEITOS: Tell me, what's going to happen?

LUSIMAKHOS: Philippos! Sometimes a doctor is necessary for Hymenios.

GUARD: Philippos!

(PHILIPPOS enters.)

PHILIPPOS: Is someone ill?

LUSIMAKHOS: Aphrodisiacs in large quantities. And, as near as I can see, you need some first. But don't worry. Kallisthenes!

GUARD: Kallisthenes!

KALLISTHENES: I'm ready, my Lord.

LUSIMAKHOS: Today you look more lively with your weighty tome guarding history.

KALLISTHENES: I've finished, sir, the last campaigns.

LUSIMAKHOS: I know. But are you, yourself, prepared.

KALLISTHENES: For recording the continuation? I've not enough papyrus . . .

LUSIMAKHOS: Not papyrus! Something else that you no longer have.

KALLISTHENES: That I no longer have? What don't I have?

LUSIMAKHOS: What you greatly need.

KALLISTHENES: I don't understand.

LUSIMAKHOS: Hymen . . . You know what that is.

KALLISTHENES: I'm not illiterate. I've read about it.

LUSIMAKHOS: And Hymenios?

KALLISTHENES: The Hymenal joy, of course.

LUSIMAKHOS: Are you prepared for that?

KALLISTHENES: Of course. I've prepared everything . . .

(General laughter.)

KALLISTHENES: . . . for recording it. Our Lord and Roxanne . . .

LUSIMAKHOS: We're talking about your own Hymenal joy.

KALLISTHENES: My own? Oh, that was a long time ago, sir.

LUSIMAKHOS: What if you had a new one? If, perhaps . . .

KLEITOS: With a shower of gold. (*Guffaws.*)

KALLISTHENES: Well . . . I'd have to collect all my thoughts to remember what I'm expected to do. But I—as far as I know—have no part in the events.

LUSIMAKHOS: Read the events. Your events kept under lock and key.

KALLISTHENES: Yes, this is how it goes. Aristotle taught Alexander to treat the Greeks and the Macedonians as if they were his brothers, but to deal with and make use of all who are not Greeks and Macedonians, but Persians and other barbarians as if they were beasts or plants. Alexander, however, deviated from his master's teaching and built his empire on the wise idea of uniting the various peoples: ecumenicity, synchronicity—these became his basic tenets used in order to eliminate the dangerous multiplicity of the conquered peoples.

KLEITOS: We know that.

LUSIMAKHOS: Read what happened tomorrow morning.

KALLISTHENES: Differently from Aristotle's teaching which was also influenced by Thales' philosophy, Alexander—after the day when griffins took him to heaven's heights— introduced a new spirit in the empire which afterward he gracefully ruled to the farthest limit of human age, and in his divine quality he practiced control over thousands of years. His human will worked through the invisible strength of Zeus-Amon's son in history which found refuge between his unchangingly strong hands.

DEMETRIOS: That's nice: "history which found refuge between his unchangingly strong hands." It's nicely written.

LUSIMAKHOS: Old man, the events will find you here by the time you tell them to us.

KALLISTHENES: The glorious sun went down from over Suza, when its son, the triumphant, young Sun-God , sanctified by Amon's priests. . . (*His words are drowned out by the spectral strong echoing sounds of crashing cymbals. The door of the throne room opens. Soldiers enter carrying Alexander's statue. After them enter Egyptian Priests. PARMENION arrives last with a robe on his arm. All present bow down falling to the earth. PARMENION remains standing. The Priests sanctify the statue, then march to the back of the stage.*)

PARMENION: It is finished. The human being who was within reach of a handshake is no more. In front of the throne of Zeus-Amon's son and the legal descendant of the pharaohs, a black carpet shows where we have to stop when approaching the mighty presence. In front of an invisible chasm. It's not true that statues don't talk. While they're standing, they keep forming opinions night and day about those who erected them. When they tumble down, about those who pulled them down. Go on. (*He puts the robe on the statue's pedestal.*) That was his. His who I could call "Alexander." Good bye, Alexander . . .

(Crash of brass cymbals. The people rise. The Egyptian Priests march out.)

LUSIMAKHOS: Go on, old man. I told you that the events would find you here.

KALLISTHENES: . . . to the triumphant young Sun God was led Roxanne of Baktria, the beautiful wife of the defeated Darius. After that in an awareness of his divine mission, he endeavored to weld together the peoples of his empire, to lift the Greek language above all, because in the vicinity of a ruling language, every other language is a secret. As such, a hiding place for private opinions, conspiracy; a false voice in the worship of gods; an obstacle in fulfilling commands. As the example of Babel shows: it's impossible to rise up to the sky when discordant speech makes construction tools clash, because the words unknown to each other beat about like wild birds. That was Zeus's punishment a long time ago. Now Zeus's son has taken away the punishment. Because where the speech is not united . . .

LUSIMAKHOS: We know it, old man! We know about Babel, foreign languages barking, Thales, ecumenicity, synchronicity, griffins, noble ideas. Tell us the facts: what happened to us tomorrow at sunrise?

KALLISTHENES: I'd tell you, but if you keep interrupting me . . .

LUSIMAKHOS: There are many of us involved.

KALLISTHENES: One of the manifestations of this effort of His was that huge wedding feast which our Lord arranged in Suza. At His command, His governors: Kleitos, Demetrios, Lusimakhos,

39

and Parmenion, the court doctor Philippos, and the generals married the daughters of the Persian nobility. Their example was followed, on Alexander's command, by more than ten thousand Grecian and Macedonian soldiers on the night of the same day.

(In the palace courts armies march, commands are given, drums sound.)

KALLISTHENES: The bridegrooms are arriving!

LUSIMAKHOS: Whom did I marry?

KALLISTHENES: Lusimakhos . . . Persephone, the daughter of the Persian satrap Massageta . . .

DEMETRIOS: Demetrios?

KALLISTHENES: Suzia, the daughter of the satrap Bessos.

KLEITOS: And Kleitos?

KALLISTHENES: Ariane, the daughter of the satrap Gaumata. You have seen all of them as they paraded in and out.

DEMETRIOS: And Parmenion, our Lord's friend, after he took the poison, who was the healing potion . . . ?

PARMENION: I forbid it! Why are you, Demetrios, so interested in it?

DEMETRIOS: Well, only . . . as a friend . . . out of joy and sympathy . . .

PARMENION: Thank you. Then hear it from me: Parmenion—refusing to obey the command, did not marry anyone.

KLEITOS: Then let's hear at least whom he didn't marry!

KALLISTHENES: Eanna, the daughter of Betis.

KLEITOS: She brought him the water of life. (*Long silence.*)

DEMETRIOS: Please, Parmenion, forgive me.

PARMENION: I've nothing to forgive.

DEMETRIOS: In appearance your would-be wife . . .

PARMENION: Not would-be!

DEMETRIOS: I committed violence against your appointed wife-by-the-command-of-our-Lord, but KLEITOS: and two soldiers can testify that . . .

PARMENION: I'm not interested!

DEMETRIOS: . . . it was only a compulsory strip search as a test, in our Lord's interest.

KLEITOS: She was suspicious.

PARMENION: Suspicious. In what way?

DEMETRIOS: In the way that . . . her stubbornness . . . her hatred obvious even from a distance . . .

PARMENION: Let me see that stubbornness . . .

DEMETRIOS: Bring in EANNA!

VOICE OF THE PALACE GUARD: Eanna!

PARMENION: . . . and that hatred. Your eagle eyes were probably not mistaken.

(EANNA enters with the Master of Ceremonies who bows and then retires to the back of the stage.)

PARMENION: So you're Eanna, the daughter of Betis?

EANNA: That's me, Sir. But I've already been searched. From you I ask only for mercy . . .

LUSIMAKHOS: You can hope only for good words from him. He will be your lord. Your husband.

(They look at one another. EANNA takes a step backward.)

PARMENION: Don't be afraid. That's only stupid talk. What have they done to you?

EANNA: What the victorious cowards always do, Sir. They humiliated me.

DEMETRIOS: Slander! It's not true! It's not true!

KLEITOS: We have witnesses, too. Captain of the Guards!

(FOURTH SOLDIER enters running.)

DEMETRIOS: And the other?

KLEITOS: Let Ali come.

FOURTH SOLDIER: He ran away, I beg to report to you.

KLEITOS: Ali ran away, and why?

FOURTH SOLDIER: He started crying, I beg to report, and then he ran away.

KLEITOS: Horsemen after him, and you, tell me you castrato: when you did that strip search, was that young woman hurt?

FOURTH SOLDIER: Not at all, I beg to report!

EANNA (*to PARMENION*): They tore off all my clothes, sir!

FOURTH SOLDIER: We'd received orders, I beg to report!

DEMETRIOS: Do you realize that he's castrated?

PARMENION: Are you trying to prove with his lack that you have—some consideration? (*To the Soldier*) You may leave.

FOURTH SOLDIER: May I leave, governor?

PARMENION: I've said that you may leave. Do you still keep on with your questioning? You have a hard head. It seems that when you were castrated they threw you away by mistake and what remained is what they cut off. Get out of here!

(FOURTH SOLDIER exits quickly.)

KLEITOS: You're over-reaching yourself, Parmenion!

PARMENION: No more than you did against this young woman.

DEMETRIOS (*placatingly*): If you don't want to marry her, why defend her?

PARMENION: I want to defend her—by not marrying her. On command I will requisition food, weapons, clothes, but not a wife. (*To EANNA*) Why are you looking at me with hatred?

EANNA: You've taken away our treasures, you've divided our lands among yourselves, you've pulled down the statues of our gods left them face-down in the ground so they shouldn't be able to talk, isn't that enough for you? Do you want to settle down in the womb of Persia?

DEMETRIOS: We should have searched her throat.

KLEITOS: Her throat is full of poison vials and daggers.

43

PARMENION: Why do you talk like that to me?

EANNA: Not to you, Sir, excuse me, but to all of you.

DEMETRIOS: When she becomes the whore of my soldiers, she'll quiet down.

PARMENION: Alexander's illusions are more noble than your filth.

DEMETRIOS: Don't forget your words!

PARMENION (*to EANNA*): Go in peace.

EANNA: Sir . . . Parmenion . . . you won't let the soldiers . . .? You all have sisters . . . I saw what the soldiers did when they were given their freedom plunde r . . . It was awful. . . . Don't punish me! If I said something wrong, forgive me. . . . You forgive me, Parmenion. To you I owe only thanks . . . (*She grabs and kisses PARMENION's hand.*)

PARMENION: I'm not a god. Go in peace.

(*EANNA exits with the Master of Ceremonies.*)

KALLISTHENES: I want your further attention, please.

PARMENION: You have it!

KALLISTHENES: And the great wedding feast at Suza filled the whole Empire with the merriment of ten thousand Hellenic bridegrooms and Persian brides. There has not been and there won't be a similarly syncretic and happy moment for humankind. Thales' prayer resounded in unison in the mixed tongues. Alexander was tireless in dancing and making use of the wine cup, but he forbade the bridegrooms to become drunk in view of the hymenal duties awaiting them. Yet many of them lost their virility. But Alexander forgave them, and on the occasion of the early morning survey—as also in earlier ecumenical weddings—he himself converted into women those who remained virgins. According to the law of nature, then, in due course, the children of the new order were born, with the signs of Hellenic beauty on their sweet faces; the earthly mirror shards of Isis and Mithras with the undeniable features of the wonderful Nike. As an expression of his unconditional obeisance to Alexander, Darius himself attended the Royal Wedding, giving up his hope for going into hiding and opposition. BETIS followed his King, Darius, on the same day at the cockcrow of dawn, and acknowledged with a reconciled heart his daughter Eanna's marriage to Parmenion who has withstood so many tests of faith. In the blessing of many children they lived happily . . . (*Long silence.*)

PARMENION: And they lived happily . . .

KALLISTHENES: The chronicle is finished for the moment.

PARMENION: What if all of that didn't happen as it will happen?

KALLISTHENES: He knows what has to happen.

PARMENION: He knew. As long as he served the facts and was able to wait for the favorable signs of everything.

KLEITOS and DEMETRIOS: And he does not know any longer?

PARMENION: He doesn't know. He dictates the future into the chronicle. He dictates his feverish dreams to Kallisthenes. This divinity is a blind alley. At the end we'll get into the guts of those whom we want to devour. Because we're hungry even when we're full.

KLEITOS: It's my duty to defend Alexander's wisdom!

DEMETRIOS: All of you must witness: I refuse to accept these calumnies!

PARMENION (*quietly*): How long has anxiety been called "calumny?"

DEMETRIOS: On the side of Zeus-Amon's son there's no anxiety, uncertainty, there's no anguish, fear, no nightmarish visions, and dissension is impossible. Although I've uttered it, this word does not exist, it's unknown, it was left at Pella, we've forgotten it, all of us, and forever. Dissension? Put knives under your pillows to kill it, even in your dreams!

LUSIMAKHOS: My friends, let's not go for each other's throats. We accept every word of our Lord without any doubt. Parmenion is tortured by doubts, but is it in his own personal interest? No, it's for Alexander, although needless, thus mistaken. But I ask you: which of us would've been able to pass the poison test for our Lord? And I ask you: isn't it possible that the medicine he took as a test was different from what cured our Lord?

PHILIPPOS: I protest! It's a calumny!

DEMETRIOS: I still suspect that Parmenion wouldn't speak like that if he were in his right mind.

PARMENION: Please don't think I'm mad.

LUSIMAKHOS: Just upset. These days anger doesn't testify that you're in your right mind. At such times as these slips of the tongue occur—but not of faithfulness, of course. For example, we don't want to devour the Persians, but generously take them into ourselves. That's our strategy to take them in.

PARMENION: Where the heart and soul are the secret catacombs?

LUSIMAKHOS: Heart and soul. Are you missing them? Look out of the window. The young women are coming by the thousands. Their parents are bringing them.

PARMENION: Because they need the tax deduction.

LUSIMAKHOS: That's our Lord's most ingenious idea, a tax deduction in the case of an ecumenical marriage.

KLEITOS: Look Parmenion, how the resistance of heart and soul, the secret catacombs, crumbles.

PARMENION: Seemingly.

KLEITOS: Under the pressure of self-interest.

LUSIMAKHOS: Because heart, soul, and sensitivity are the three little servants of material interest, of promotion, and of every kind of benefit. Do you hear? They're even singing.

PARMENION: Not a song of joy.

DEMETRIOS: They sing the same when they marry among themselves. The pretended sadness before the marriage night.

LUSIMAKHOS (*at the window*): Parmenion, you poetic soul! Look at the Persian peasant, how he giggles with the Greek soldier. Like the man at Megara in Aristophanes: shall I sell you, my daughters, or will you go on starving? Sell us. Sell us! But how? It doesn't matter, perhaps disguised as pigs in a bag. Do you recall how Dikaipolis felt them by touching? They've no tails! They'll have them when they're bigger, big thick and red tails, but just feel them in the front—they're already getting fat and furry. They'll make two nice snacks for Aphrodite. (*Laughs.*) the man from Megara, the one from Baktria—if the daughters' father gets cornered then morality doesn't matter.

PARMENION: Doesn't matter.

DEMETRIOS (*from the window*): They're already shaking hands. The happy father doesn't calculate that although he gives only one daughter, he gives with her in the next generation a whole division of soldiers. If she bears only seven children and they each produce the same number for the Empire, seven times seven and that multiplied again . . . just count how many newly produced Hellenic soldiers and how many breeding places. One silky and hot little mound of Venus that fits in a palm. Our Lord knows all that well, and you doubt it.

PARMENION: I've known about your monomania, Demetrios. As for your erotomania, I'm just beginning to notice it.

DEMETRIOS: It's certainly healthier than your Narcissism! Or perhaps it's not yourself, but another man who's the object of your love?

(*Rough laughter except for KALLISTHENES.*)

ALEXANDER'S VOICE: Parmenion! Send my friend, Parmenion, here at once!

A GUARD: Zeus-Amon's Son wants Parmenion!

(Frozen silence.)

PARMENION: Continue! Guffawing and grunting. Because I think that this aggressive social climbing has given you the sensitive nose of a wild boar! This mad rush around Alexander. My words have the smell of opposition and already you've caught the sent—and you defend Him against me. You would only need a signal to tear me in pieces while still alive. Not out of faithfulness to him, you all know that well enough, don't you, you who are not guffawing any more. It's that pitiable but all the more fanatic hatred that's working in you because of the friendship between the two of us. What can I do so that he should love you more? Don't lie to him. Perhaps he knows that you lie when you flatter him—and perhaps he knows that I'm the most attached to him when I refuse his orders. He reached after me a hundred times when I fell—and I'll reach a thousand times after him if his eyes start to dazzle from his own glory and he stumbles again and again. Because friendship is two bodies and one soul. But to whom am I talking?

ALEXANDER'S VOICE: Parmenion!

PARMENION: I'm coming, stop yelling! If somebody is a god at least they shouldn't yell. *(Quick exit.)*

DEMETRIOS: I'll be a dog if he hasn't lost his right mind, Philippos.

(Third trumpet sounds.)

KLEITOS: Guards! Open the eastern gate!

LUSIMAKHOS: Master of Ceremonies, the young women!

(The GUARDS exit in the indicated direction, drums sound outside, on the command: "Soldiers! Everybody take their bride to the site of the feast! Hurrah!" The Master of Ceremonies leads in the young women among them SUZIA, Persephone, Ariane, EANNA, as the music in the background grows louder. He brings the women one by one to stand next to their appointed men. The young women bring trays with glass chalices filled with wine which the men drink and then smash one by one against the wall. The Master of Ceremonies collects the trays and carries them off stage. EANNA stands alone and off to the side.)

DEMETRIOS: Roxanne arrives. Guards, salute!

(From the side the voice of the invisible guards): Glory to Alexander, may the Hellenic Empire live forever! (ROXANNE: arrives with her entourage. The three Governors greet her silently.)

ROXANNE: Glory to Alexander, the Son of the Sun God, and so forth. And the new Queen? Or has Thales' prayer excluded me, too, from respect? From today onward Roxanne will be your ruler and Captain, who will bear a son, a legal successor to Alexander so that this whole concoction from the Adriatic to India . . .

DEMETRIOS: But, my Queen . . .

ROXANNE: . . . should survive! And Roxanne shouldn't live? The Empire will fall to pieces if there's no successor out of her womb. I leave Darius, so that on the invitation of Alexander I share the cares of reigning and you miserable slaves, you've no word of greeting for me.

BESSOS: Long Live Roxanne. (*He comes forward with a silk bag under his arm.*)

ROXANNE: Are you also here BESSOS? We missed you.

BESSOS: I'm late, your majesty, but I'm here . . .

KLEITOS: We apologize to the great Darius's widow . . .

ROXANNE: I'm not a widow. Darius is alive and is going to give his right hand in peace to Alexander. They're not enemies any longer, they've always highly esteemed one another.

LUSIMAKHOS: That's what we heard, also.

KLEITOS: I'm sorry your Highness: we haven't received instructions about how to greet you. Guards! Glory to the Queen!

VOICE OF THE GUARDS: Glory to Alexander! May The Hellenic Empire Live Forever!

DEMETRIOS: And our lady, Roxanne.

ROXANNE (*laughs*): Parrots. The living examples of training. You'll learn the new greeting, too. The one for the couple. You dried up collection of bachelors, you'll learn that there's also a woman in the palace—the lawful wife of the world conqueror, Alexander. You've each received a woman and you should be able to keep up with them. These are not pale nymphs, my good lords, and they are not modestly weaving Penelopes. Their blood is somewhat more spicey in case you don't know, my lords. Look at them! My daughters, I hope you're not being sad in the very first minute of the Suza wedding! In my Persepolis court you were songbirds. Persephone, Ariane, Suzia . . . and where is Eanna? Come here, my daughter. (*EANNA goes to ROXANNE*) Don't grieve. All of you, be beautiful like the hanging gardens of Semiramis, fertile like the Valley of the Nile; be peaceful like the doves, and smart like the snakes. What bad fate brought us we'll turn to our benefit. What the men lost with weapons we'll regain with love. Darius won't be the King of Persia any longer, but Alexander has offered him his friendship and is going to share power with him. The same way with our old satraps. Look, Bessos is here and he'll continue governing Baktria. Now, go to your husbands. Hey Bessos! Compared to the generosity of Alexander your gift looks small with which you wish to express your homage. Or perhaps you're bringing pure gold in your silk bag?

BESSOS: With what I brought, my Lady, Alexander won't be richer, but no doubt his sleep will be less disturbed.

ROXANNE: As always: your reply is cunning, Bessos. But why doesn't Alexander come? Or shall I have to present myself to him? (*The doors of the throne room open.*)

KLEITOS: Alexander arrives! Guards!

THE VOICE OF THE GUARDS: Glory to Alexander!

(*PARMENION enters.*)

PARMENION: Your ladyship, I receive you on behalf of Alexander. He sends his loving greeting and expects you inside. You alone! He isn't going to accept the homage of the satraps until morning.

BESSOS: We've brought a gift! I have!

PARMENION: I've been given the right to accept it. The gift goes before the giver. Although it is brought by satraps, every pearl and whatever else it could be is to be the wedding gift to the Queen. There, please. (*He points to a table. While the members of ROXANNE's entourage put down their wedding gifts, PARMENION goes on with his speech of welcome.*) I must say on command of Alexander, Roxanne the gods have led you on your voluntarily chosen path towards the marriage bed of universal reconciliation. May general harmony be fulfilled in our empire with the fruit of your womb. Although you should know from Plato who says, referring to Heraclitus: harmony is created out of contrasting elements like rhythm in music—but you're not interested in that now. Lead us, together with Alexander, out of the beggar-like sundriness of so many peoples towards the unity of the Hellenic spirit. I'm saying this—on His command and in spite of my own conviction.

ROXANNE: So Alexander sent my enemy in his place to meet me.

PARMENION: His friend, my Lady, whom he's always allowed to think what he wants, but publicly say what he must. Now is such a case, with a little modification on my part: I'm saying the two together. Both what I think and what I must.

(DEMETRIOS whispers something to ROXANNE.)

ROXANNE: According to the signs, slow poison speaks from you. One takes off his mask before his death.

PARMENION: As long as Alexander lives, I live, too.

ROXANNE: May the gods grant it.

BESSOS: My Lord! I can give my gift only in person to Alexander himself.

PARMENION: Impossible.

BESSOS: In person and in private.

PARMENION: All the more impossible.

BESSOS: I can't give it into anyone else's hands.

PARMENION: I'm not anyone else's hand. I've known since Troy that every gift is suspicious, even Persian fidelity.

BESSOS: I can't give it. I'd rather leave. *(He begins to exit.)*

ROXANNE: BESSOS! Every gift is my gift! I order you to open that bag.

BESSOS: No . . . I can't do that . . .

(PARMENION takes the bag from him. He pulls out the head of Darius, then lets it drop back into the bag. First frozen silence then screams from ROXANNE: and the women.)

ROXANNE: Assassin! *(As if escaping from Darius's severed head.)* Assassin! Bessos, you Assassin! O Darius!—you in your credulity were nurturing your murderer. You were paying your murderers expensive gold and confidence! Darius you, the most stupid of all kings. You should've trusted only your enemies—their intention is always clear. Bessos why did you do that? Why?

BESSOS: I cannot serve two kings.

ROXANNE: You cannot! You damned! He who serves one falsely—can serve two! O Persians! My sisters and brothers! Is there not a man among you who would revenge Darius on this rat? You Greeks, Macedonians! Alexander's friend, noble counterpart . . . will nobody avenge his death?

PARMENION: The right of judgment is only His.

ROXANNE: O Alexander! Do not leave it unpunished. (*She collapses on EANNA's shoulders.*)

EANNA: He who serves one falsely—can serve two. He who loves one falsely—can love two, also. Be beautiful like the hanging gardens of Semiramis. What bad fate brought us, let us turn to our benefit.

ROXANNE (*madly*): Eanna, is that you—Eanna?

EANNA: It's me, Eanna.

ROXANNE: You're speaking strange words.

EANNA: A queen said them. Whose hair I combed in Persepolis.

ROXANNE: Her hair. In Persepolis. I was waiting for Darius under the cedars. The sun has set, my darling, get up and be the light. He always came on a black horse. What happened to Darius's black horses?

PARMENION: My lady, Alexander is waiting for you.

55

ROXANNE: What happened to Darius's black horses?

EANNA: Forgive me.

PARMENION: We must go.

ROXANNE: Where must we go?

PARMENION: Our Lord is waiting. Alexander.

ROXANNE: Our Lord is waiting. Alexander. (*Takes the bag away from PARMENION.*) Our Lord, Alexander. (*Seizing PARMENION's arm, she goes towards the throne room.*) Our Lord, Alexander . . . (*At the door she collapses. She just drags herself further. The doors close. PARMENION does not go in, but searches for EANNA with his eyes.*)

DEMETRIOS: Kleitos, Lusimakhos! Our wedding march!

(*Those who are present—with the exception of BESSOS who has collapsed into himself—sing aloud Thales' prayer: "The gods be praised" etc. They dance. From the whirling crowd Ariane, SUZIA, Persephone, stretch out their hands from time to time to EANNA to include her, from time to time some men's hands also grab her.*)

EANNA: Curse you! Curse you! Curse you!

PARMENION (*slowly goes towards EANNA and stops her mouth with his hand*): Be quiet!

EANNA (*shouts in his face*): A curse on you!

CURTAIN

act two

(BETIS' castle. Men, Women, and Children with
their heads and hands on the ground. First, the
Suza wedding music is heard, then the wordless
lamentation of the castle inhabitants which
grows stronger. BETIS and YOUNG BESSOS
stand in the foreground, the former as rigid as
a statue. YOUNG BESSOS repairing his
weapon.)

A WOMAN'S VOICE: Betis, pray!

BETIS: It's weapons we need. That is, we would
need . . .

A WOMAN'S VOICE: Betis, pray to the gods for
help.

BETIS: They don't have weapons.

A WOMAN'S VOICE: Our priests have deserted us,
Betis! Pray!

BETIS: I won't pray. The priests know very well
when to shut up. When the sky is deserted.
Like the house emptied by murdering thieves.

A MAN'S VOICE: Betis, Young Bessos! Pray. If
there's still a god, he'd listen to your words.

BETIS: The faces of Isis and Mithras are mired in
mud. They've fallen face down on the ground.
Shall I pray to the new gods? To Zeus, Apollo,

Nike? I don't speak Greek and they won't be such fools as to help us. It wasn't us that fed them.

YOUNG BESSOS: Instead of complaints, people expect consolation from you. Yes. Darius will at last collect the scattered armies. My father also has left North Baktria. The Maccabees have risen up against the Macedonians and the Syrians will follow their example, the Medes . . .

BETIS: They're all a long way away.

YOUNG BESSOS: You can find encouraging signs nearer also.

BETIS: Eanna? Your sister, Suzia? Mrs. Parmenion, Mrs. Demetrios? You still don't believe that about them? Anyway, they're allowed to do what they want. We don't have our god any longer to punish them. We're growing rotten from the inside out. If we want have any chance at all, then we have to cut off our own limbs.

YOUNG BESSOS: The young bitch follows the older one.

BETIS: Don't talk like that.

YOUNG BESSOS: Roxanne.

BETIS: We'll even things out with her.

YOUNG BESSOS: We'll even her out! So you do have hope!

A WOMAN'S VOICE: Betis, pray!

YOUNG BESSOS: So far you've kept our spirits alive, now you've no right to be despondent— because of women's treachery.

BETIS: Shall I tell you what the solace is? Shall I tell you what the reality is? About the massacred troglodytes? The mole's status of those who escaped to the mountains? Our children in new cities bereft of their mothers' language? In the Alexandrias where they're the ones who make the laws and we execute them? They're the inspectors and we the inspected; they're the designers of lighthouses and we're the porters of luggage, the waiters carrying food, the gravediggers, and the garbage men? And shall I tell you the most woeful thing of all? In the conquered regions, even the once straight backbones have been cooked soft in just a few years with the help of tax deductions. And I'm not talking about the women, they're accomplices of the gods old and new. When a new god is born, he first counts on the women.

YOUNG BESSOS: Now it's my turn to say don't speak like that, my brother. Don't slander the women of your own castle.

BETIS: I ask their pardon, if I do. Personal loss is always the all-in-all. What good is a little consolation, if you can't take part in it?

VOICES: Betis, Young Bessos! Pray.

BETIS: Mithras at the moment is being repulsed by the Suza wedding feast.

YOUNG BESSOS: Help him in his repulsion.

BETIS: Only curses grow in my throat.

YOUNG BESSOS: You're our leader until Darius and my father arrive.

BETIS: Mithras got up from the mire, Isis got up from the clay. They're enjoying themselves together with Nike at Suza. Perhaps they're already drunk . . . they vomit the prayers of two thousand years.

VOICES: Blasphemer! God slanderer!

(A man leaves the crowd and brandishes a knife against BETIS.)

THE MAN: Pray for us, or you'll be silent forever!

(YOUNG BESSOS knocks him down.)

BETIS: You can pray yourself.

THE MAN: It's not a question of me, a miserable water-carrier, but of us!

YOUNG BESSOS: They entrusted you with the use of the plural. We entrusted you with our words.

BETIS (*to THE MAN who tried to attack him with the knife*): You know that my daughter, Eanna, followed Roxanne and in spite of that?

THE MAN: In spite of that, my Lord! In spite of that!

YOUNG BESSOS: All the more reason for you to name the trouble, if you can't give voice to consolation. That also gives strength.

VOICES: Betis, pray!

BETIS: It gives strength. It gives strength.

> If we say whole country went insane,
> God has deserted us,
> The whole country became confused.
> The city whose Lord doesn't care . . ..
> The city is crying aloud,
> Weeping, it laments.
> Its guardian wails,
> Its shepherd plays a mournful flute.
>
> . . . .

Even the keening priest does not beseech:
"Let your heart find peace."
Our Lord is no longer staying with us,
Our Lady is no longer staying with us:
Our Lord has thundered into the mountains,
Our Lady has thundered into the mountains.
The kit fox bites his own tail,The wild hen cries out in fright. Those outside are seized by a whirlwind,Those inside are also seized by a whirlwind, Those outside are scattered by a hurricane, Those inside are scattered by grievous destruction.

. . . .

What has the Lord decided in his heart?
What has the Lord decided in his mind?
With His Holy Reason of what did the Lord think?
He flooded the empire with destruction.
He planted barren weeds in the fields.
Like blighted corn seeds
He scattered black-headed men in the fields.
O, Enlil, the country is lost!
O, Father Enlil the country is lost!
Why did You bless this land so richly before,
If now You intend to let it fall into ruin?
Why did You call people to arms,
If now they throw away their swords?

(EANNA enters, stops, the look on her face says: my father lives.)

61

Implacable, terrible, vengeful God!
Sitting in ashes we beseech You—
Relent in Your anger,
And sign our letter of absolution!

A WOMAN'S VOICE: Hardhearted, terrible, vengeful God!

THE CROWD: Sign our letter of absolution.

BETIS: Go, people go now!

(All exit except YOUNG BESSOS and BETIS. BETIS embraces EANNA without a word.)

EANNA: My dear father . . .

BETIS: Did the prayer bring you? I didn't believe . . . I don't believe . . . Eanna! (*With an outburst of joy.*) Eanna! Don't cry. You must tell us all. How did you escape?

YOUNG BESSOS: And my father? And how is Suzia?

BETIS: And Darius?

EANNA: As many questions as many assaults upon us.

BETIS: How did you escape?

EANNA: With a letter of safe conduct from Parmenion.

BETIS: Parmenion? At what price?

YOUNG BESSOS: Where did Suzia: stay?

BETIS: With the letter of a Macedonian . . . at what price?

YOUNG BESSOS: And why alone?

BETIS: At what price?

EANNA: He doesn't want me.

BETIS: No. Was it his decision only?

EANNA: Perhaps it was mine as well.

BETIS: Perhaps? Only perhaps?

EANNA: If you must know: not perhaps. Certainly it was both of ours.

YOUNG BESSOS: My brother, don't examine your daughter's honor now. Where's my father with the rescuing army? Where is Suzia?

BETIS: Young Bessos, remember: the rescuing army and my daughter's honor are not mutually exclusive.

EANNA: Suzia is Demetrios's wife. There's no rescuing army, no Darius and no Bessos, although I saw him alive—with the King's severed head. He took it in a silk bag to Alexander as a gift.

YOUNG BESSOS: Who are you talking about? What are you saying?

EANNA: That's the truth.

YOUNG BESSOS: My father? Bessos? The King's head in a silk bag . . .!

BETIS: You're coming from horror, you're confused, my daughter.

YOUNG BESSOS: Confused? Bribed! With Parmenion's letter of safe conduct—and on what kind of errand? That you should break our resistance with lies and rumors?

BETIS: Don't blame her! They've misled you, Eanna.

EANNA: I saw it with my own two eyes.

YOUNG BESSOS: My father—with the King's head? I'll kill him. Regicide cries out for patricide. But it can't be true! You came as the Greeks' pander . . . you're despicable!

EANNA: My father! Don't tolerate his dirty accusations!

YOUNG BESSOS: ". . . Like blighted corn seeds . . ."

BETIS: I won't tolerate it. But what was the price of your freedom?

EANNA: I've told you.

YOUNG BESSOS: "He scattered black-headed men in the fields . . ."

BETIS: What was the price of your freedom?

YOUNG BESSOS: What you're saying is frightful. You're lying!

BETIS: What was the price of your freedom? Tell me!

(PARMENION is led in by two guards.)

EANNA: Here he is! Let him speak!

GUARD: I beg to report to you: this Macedonian claims he's Alexander's personal Messenger.

BETIS You may leave. (*Exit guards.*) Speak.

PARMENION: Yes, it's me, Parmenion.

BETIS: Didn't we meet in Athens? Then we were the victors.

PARMENION: Then you burnt the Acropolis.

BETIS: And you now are burning Persepolis.

PARMENION: We, although that's not quite the correct word.

EANNA: He isn't.

BETIS: There are situations where the singular pronoun ceases to exist.

PARMENION: In times of war only the first and second plural persons exist, sir, that is: we and you.

YOUNG BESSOS: Stop chattering! You Macedonian! Did you also see Darius's severed head?

PARMENION: Yes, I saw it. Also Bessos.

YOUNG BESSOS: I'll kill him. I'll even throw away my name and let it be cursed in this country forever.

BETIS: And where is the country, my son?

YOUNG BESSOS: Where is the country? Not one square foot remains where such a curse could be effective. Where shall I go? Where can I hide myself as the son of a cowardly murderer? Tell me, Betis. . . . Tell me, Eanna!

EANNA: I've no word for your despair, Bessos.

YOUNG BESSOS: Despair? There's no word to describe it.

BETIS: None. All that we own is in a realm where there's no word for it.

YOUNG BESSOS: What can I now put in my prayer to the skies?

> Our Lord, thou avenger!
> Our Lord, thou destroyer!
> Hardhearted, terrible vengeful God!
> . . . .
> He made my heart weak,
> He tangled my arms around me,
> . . . .
> He scourged me with the anger of the country
> He tore my name from out of the people's

mouths.
My Lord, I cry out to you,
Let my cry come unto Thee!

Let my cry come unto Thee!
Thou deservest to have been thrown
down into the mud!
Thou deservest it!
Thou art indifferent and a betrayer!

BETIS: Bessos, my son.

EANNA: Bessos. Try to calm down.

YOUNG BESSOS: O, I don't even know what I'm
saying. Like one whose two wings are cut off.
My father . . . Suzia . . . Suzia . . . Mrs.
Demetrios: . . . Who was the girl who grew up
beside me . . .? Who was the man who brought
me up? Tell me! Tell me something!

EANNA: Come, come, Bessos . . .

YOUNG BESSOS: Where? From nothing to nothing!
From a lie . . . from an illusion, that—there
were three of us? (*EANNA leads him off.*)
Three of us . . . and what remains of us. . . .
What remains of us! (*They exit. Distant sounds
of the wedding march.*)

BETIS: Why did you come?

PARMENION: With Alexander's proposal.

BETIS: We don't have any more kings whose heads
I could bring him. And I've only one daughter
whom they wanted for the communal wedding
bed. I thank you for my daughter.

PARMENION: She cursed me. I hope it won't take.
But right now that's not the point. You can't
hold the castle any longer. You surely know
that.

BETIS: I know. And yet . . .

PARMENION: Alexander . . . Alexandros now offers you through me safe conduct for the third time.

BETIS: To where?

PARMENION: I don't know. I'm not from around here.

BETIS: But I am, and I know the end of the route of safe conduct. Those who laid down their weapons quickly began to transform their faces. Our nobles, our satraps. In the name of our people . . . say the jackals. But where is the people? On the gallows.

PARMENION: Don't exaggerate. There are many of them at the great wedding feast.

BETIS: O yes, at the wedding. Daughters and widows of nobles in the palace of Suza.

PARMENION: And those of tradesmen, peasants, and little clerks in the towns and villages. More than ten thousand of them.

BETIS: Yet someone's missing from there.

PARMENION: Eanna.

BETIS: She, too. But what did you see, Parmenion? Your bridegrooms and our daughters executing the Order of the Day. Those dragged there by the hair of their head, those who were openly or secretly prostitutes, and those miserable rats of brides' fathers motivated by the tax deduction. You didn't see those who were carefully beaten to death by the suitors at the happy occasion of their proposing—because they resisted.

PARMENION: That's the exception. And in your place I wouldn't deceive myself so much with the idea of resistance.

BETIS: I don't deny it: you can already count the tax deduction promised to the brides' fathers as one of your gods. Its power sometimes surpasses that of the spirit, of language, and all the heritage of the ancestors. But even if there isn't open resistance, somebody's missing from there. Somebody with a double name: Love and Free Will.

PARMENION: I know. Force and necessity are invisible on the surface. Did you think I would contradict you?

BETIS: I thought of something else. It's strange that you can imagine yourself in our skin.

PARMENION: I'm not sure it does me any good.

BETIS: My daughter was your prisoner. Why did you free her?

PARMENION: Because of the absence of that person with the double name: Love and Free Will. Of course, on your daughter's part. (*BETIS hesitates to ask: "And how about on your part?" At last he doesn't say it.*)

BETIS: You're loved by the gods, Parmenion. That "absence" saves your life here and now. Perhaps Eanna's, also.

PARMENION: Thank you. And what if you become disappointed in me? If that absence in me were to be filled by . . .?

BETIS: I can't be disappointed in you. You're my enemy.

PARMENION: But I've brought you the message of peace. As I've said: safe conduct.

BETIS (*only playing with the idea*): And will he give me the troglodyte children collected in Suzia?

PARMENION: He won't.

BETIS: Does he want to be the benevolent father of so many Persian children?

PARMENION: And even more. Of course he wouldn't trust them to their mothers. So that they should bring them up leading them back to your cause? To your gods? So that he should always have the bother of employing informers? Those who'd inform him about—your lullabies? The Lord of the world isn't afraid of death, but believe me I know him well: he's afraid of your lullabies. (*BETIS listens a little confused and suspicious.*) Because your language and your religion, as long as you practice them, are treason, betrayal, a continuous conspiracy against us. How many billions of words does a mother waste on her child? They all influence him to be different from us—we who want him to resemble us. Or don't you know that? Childhood is the mind's slumber. Doesn't that sound good? The slumber of the mind. Well, the young person, the warrior ready to die for the empire, will belong to those who wake up the child's mind from its state of slumber for their own purposes, for themselves. Those who won't hesitate to let him know in his youth that although his father is a Macedonian soldier, his mother—was a mistake. The child has to identify himself as Macedonian, Greek, a proud Hellene. Glory to Alexandros . . .

BETIS: I thought that it was only me . . . only us, the ones concerned who knew that behind the foxy insinuations of universal order and harmony, you long for our cheese so openly; relying on our credulity.

PARMENION: Of course we won't be such fools as to awaken—or deepen your suspicion. Alexander already gives his commands to his soldiers in three languages.

BETIS: Because that way . . .

PARMENION: Don't say it, don't malign him, you still can fall into his hands. I'll say it for you: he promises a new country, but he's designing it to be a furnace. He begins in three languages so that he can continue in a single one. A clever god. He's not two-faced, not Janus-faced, but three-faced.

BETIS: Promises a new country, wants to lift us up, us dirty troglodytes—in revenge, because, as it's said, his father was killed by Darius. Do you believe that?

PARMENION: Who knows, I suspect that the cause of something is, perhaps, not necessarily identical with the motive. And in knowing this, the past is always useful for us, especially in its falsified form.

BETIS: And do you admit it so shamelessly?

PARMENION: Will you be stronger if I hide it?

BETIS: Against you Greeks—I'm becoming weaker by the moment. Militarily.

PARMENION: At last you understand.

BETIS: And yet . . .

PARMENION: What "yet?"

BETIS: Bessos. The betrayer.

PARMENION: And betrayal? Is that the "yet"?

BETIS: The mere realization. That the traitors are multiplying among us. For the moment we can't do anything against you Greeks. But against ourselves it's already clear what we must do. Have you seen Young Bessos? Through such disappointments we grow stronger.

PARMENION: Isn't that a poor solace?

BETIS: What we didn't have in us is now being born in us, the only thing that can still help—the sense of danger.

PARMENION: That's what we want to lay to rest.

BETIS: You're too open. That's your disguise.

PARMENION: I should've said the opposite of all that. I'm Alexander's friend.

BETIS: Alexander wants to make this whole miserable sleeping sea of an eastern world undulate. In place of our tents and earthen huts, there'll arise a series of glorious Alexandrine towns. There'll be roads, schools, libraries, sports stadia in the conquered territories, a million scrolls in the Library at Alexandria, and light for a hundred miles at sea from the lighthouse at Pharos, the hundred gates of Thebes, marble and gold statues by Pheidias and Praxiteles. Let's bring in trade, shipbuilding, and knowledge in place of ignorance! Worshipping the stars? In a stupid eastern way? They're common fireballs—Thales!—and these people don't even have a philosophy. Never mind, I'll have some brought to them. Plato and Aristotle! Theatre, aqueducts, medicine! And a mirror in which they can all recognize their real selves:

Aristophanes, Euripides! And how many kinds of phanes and pides!

PARMENION: Stop mocking. All that's true.

BETIS: Why don't you say so then?

PARMENION: Because in Suza I've seen the rounded-up troglodyte children and something even more painful: on the road I saw hanged men.

BETIS: You're a traitor!

PARMENION: Perhaps a deserter.

BETIS: It comes to the same thing.

PARMENION: You're thinking in extremes. Can you only conceive of fanatic believers and traitors? There can be something in between the two. That state of punishment in which I exist. As a punishment I was given my errand to communicate to you what I don't believe in.

BETIS: I don't understand you.

PARMENION: Because you don't know what happened tomorrow at sunrise. And soon the cocks will crow.

BETIS: Now I really don't understand you.

PARMENION: Thanks to his divine vision, Alexander dictates to the court historian the future—as the past. Until now he was able to do so because his intention and execution never came into conflict. As for you and me, the divine plan is now the following: Betis followed his king in tendering his submission next dawn at cockcrow, and then it continues: he accepted, with an acquiescent heart, the marriage of his daughter Eanna—to Parmenion.

BETIS: "With an acquiescent heart . . ." (*Laughs.*) Throwing his daughter after his honor. His only daughter to the Macedonian bastards. . . . And his own rear end to some Greek pederast . . .

PARMENION: Don't slander! I was talking to you man-to-man because I respected you. But I can also talk with my sword. I was talking to Betis, the man, not to a cowardly rat who only has insulting words.

BETIS: I said "bastards," not Parmenion. Bastards—in the plural.

PARMENION: But you included me, too!

BETIS: Please forgive me. After all, you gave my daughter her freedom. You're her accomplice in her escape. But if you're honest, you won't expect my gratitude for that.

PARMENION: I don't.

BETIS: And do you believe in what happened tomorrow at sunrise?

PARMENION: I've told you: I'm here because I do not. I didn't want to convince you—which would've been my task—so I can only tell you the end of the affair.

BETIS: And what is the end?

PARMENION: He'll have your ankles drilled through then you'll be dragged across town at the end of a horse's rein.

BETIS: That will be so. I'm sorry for you that you can't take a more favorable answer. Because that's what's going to happen.

PARMENION: Then you also know that he could've annihilated you long ago. Don't you suspect his patience? What he needs isn't your surrendering weapons in the face of overwhelming power. But that out of your free will. . . . That you should recognize the self-interest of the Persians.

BETIS: Our interests, of course! Be our brother, Betis, the sons of Hellas accept you; return to your right mind, Betis, the sons of Hellas share with you their power, their language, their culture, even their gods, if you throw away your barbarian identity. Be Greek, Macedonian, and with and through them you can exercise their rights as an equal. Return to your right mind, Betis, throw out of yourself Mithras, Ahriman, the god of evil. Your gods, the evil ones are good only to make you different from the Greeks. The real gods live on Mt. Olympus. If you join us and forget your barbarian name, look at how beautiful your new name will sound: instead of Betis—Philon, Plato, Xenophon, and Anakreon! You could be a voting member of the Agora and, if you deserve it, through incessantly informing on your own kind, then you could become a leader of a city state and by the time you become old you could even be a member of the highest council. (*Almost mad.*) I don't want to be a councilor! Here are my ankles, drill them through, where are the reins? Haven't you brought the torture instruments with you?

PARMENION: I've brought my doubts. Don't slander me.

BETIS Take your doubts to your Lord and tell him without doubt: Betis is not for sale. His daughter isn't for sale either! He can take everything from us by force: nothing is for sale. Go!

PARMENION: I can't go.

BETIS: Your poor pitiable soul. You can't account for it.

PARMENION: Even if you're surprised: it's difficult for me . . .

BETIS: To admit failure?

PARMENION: To accept your death by torture.

BETIS: You're sorry for me? You took pity on me! (*Laughs bitterly.*) He comes here from beside the Adriatic, he burns the country to ashes, massacres the men, rapes the women and girls—and now he's sorry for me! You gods, fallen with your faces in the earth, if you haven't gotten drowned in the mud, you can now choke with laughter! From guffawing! The Macedonian is sorry, he sheds tears . . . he's become remorseful. He's ashamed, he blushes at the sight of those hanging on the gallows, he worries about my neck, my ankles, and if they drag me with reins, he'll beg for a little cushion to put under my head. Betis, don't hit yourself on the bloody stones! Tell me Betis, did they drill through your ankles considerately and tenderly? Was your death by torture easy and comfortable, Betis? Come and lay your head on my shoulder. In the name of universal order, of general reconciliation, come and lay your head on my shoulder! The cadaver and the blushing hangman! The cadavers, and the hangmen anguished by their doubts! Shouldn't the heart break, Parmenion? I'll count my armament makers. If you like, be my guest. But the one thing you must never ask me to have: doubt.

I've no doubts. Only my hopelessness. (*Exits quickly*.)

(*Sound of distant wedding music for a few seconds. EANNA enters.*)

EANNA: I heard everything. Do something Parmenion. He's forged a weapon for himself out of hopelessness.

PARMENION: I gave myself away to him, and he abused my honesty. The obstinate and stupid untalented general without an army.

EANNA: Don't speak about him like that. He doesn't know you.

PARMENION: Why, do you know me?

EANNA: You saved my life.

PARMENION: You wouldn't have died of that. Persephone, Suzia, and the others . . . are all alive.

EANNA: I had poison on me.

PARMENION: Poison?

EANNA: Quick acting poison. Here you are. . . . (*She shows it*.) I stole it from Philippos.

PARMENION: From Philippos.

EANNA: I switched it with something similar—one of my sedatives.

PARMENION: When Philippos was going to Alexander.

EANNA: Yes.

PARMENION: And Philippos got it from Roxanne.

EANNA: From Roxanne.

PARMENION: From the cobra . . . I understand. . . .

Somebody is benevolently playing with us. Which god could it be?

EANNA: ?

PARMENION: Somebody up there's playing while down here you saved my life.

EANNA: I don't understand you.

PARMENION: You'll understand it. And what if Demetrius had found the poison on you?

EANNA: He was preoccupied. In the state of a dog in rut . . .

PARMENION: Somebody's playing with us. They would've executed you.

EANNA: How good it is now. Both of us are alive. I would've died beside you—at the sound of your wedding march. But now we're both alive.

PARMENION: We're alive. I must go.

EANNA: Don't go.

PARMENION: I must hurry to Alexander—with my failure.

EANNA: Stay a little longer.

PARMENION: All of you get away from here . . . flee. I don't want his death.

EANNA: But your people want it all the more.

PARMENION: Mine, yours! You don't have any other words! Bessos: yours? Demetrios: mine? You and us—the perennial plural. . . . Your father's the same! "A curse on you!" you alone screamed into my single face. How many persons am I to you?—to all of you? Did I parcel you out to myself? Did I throw dice for you? Did I have you strip-searched? And did you see what your Persians did in Athens to the women and to the statues of Pheideas? Shall I replace all of them with your father? The same way he treats me—mocking my doubts? Do I want him to surrender—before my most sacred appearance? Did I lose his war? Is it such awful hypocrisy on my part that I don't want to see him dragged behind a horse at the end of a rein? That I don't want to see you crying—over his corpse? Is it so difficult to understand?

EANNA: Forgive me, Parmenion. I entreat you also in his name.

PARMENION (*relenting*): He didn't authorize you to do so.

EANNA: Out of mere pride. He's ashamed to show his feelings in front of you.

PARMENION: I didn't expect him to kiss my hands.

EANNA: In his eyes—you are Alexander whatever you say or do.

PARMENION: In a silk bag—with Alexander's head I'd find more favor with him. He was a curly haired child in Pella. A miniature imitation Apollo. We amused ourselves by breaking in wild black horses. The Pella wind went whistling by our ears. Then we didn't even talk; we only laughed with each other.

EANNA: Like lovers.

PARMENION: Patroklos and Achilleus. Wearing his arms I ran as to a toy enemy below a toy Troy.

EANNA: The game became more grim.

PARMENION: He was my only friend. And that "only friend" became a God.

EANNA: You immerse yourself in the past, in the horsey days of Pella, and you'll destroy yourself.

PARMENION: Not only the past but also the future ties me up with both hands. It's called Eanna. But she's armed with poison and curses—against me.

EANNA: I was hateful; lest I should come to hate you.

PARMENION: Oracular talk.

EANNA: You said you didn't want me.

PARMENION: Lest you should be the first to refuse me. But be gracious unto me: never forgive that one sin.

EANNA: Never.

PARMENION: Let that be the only sin that I've ever committed against you.

EANNA: Your first and last sin. How stormy the sea is.

PARMENION: The sea?

EANNA: Odysseus's boat is drifting between Scylla and Carybdis. My friends now I'll block your ears with soft wax so that you won't hear the Sirens' voice and won't be destroyed. As for me, tie me to the mast, because Circe allowed me to listen to their song. . . . Please don't pity me—tighten the ropes around me!

PARMENION (*after a short amazed period he understands the game*): Direct your boat towards us, O Great Odysseus. Row your boat to us and enjoy our song!

EANNA: I entreat you—take pity on me and untie my ropes! Parmenion's waiting for me on the island. Untie my ropes! (*PARMENION unties*

79

invisible ropes from around EANNA and embraces her. The sounds of the wedding march come with brutal force from below the castle walls. EANNA freezes.)

PARMENION (*opens the window*): A new herd at the wedding feast.

EANNA: Thales' prayer—the prayer of the two of us . . .

PARMENION: We'll forget it.

EANNA: And the others?

PARMENION: They'll sing it enthusiastically.

EANNA: Mob hysteria. Shall we live among insane people, Parmenion?

PARMENION: We'll look upon them, and pass by.

EANNA: Where? O where?

PARMENION: Into our own peace.

EANNA: Into loneliness?

PARMENION: Somewhere . . . under our own sky.

EANNA: Where is it? From Athens to Egypt there is only one sky. And this wolf howling. Even our life extended into our children is only a wolf howling, Parmenion! Your . . .

VOICE OF YOUNG BESSOS: Grecian dogs! Macedonian jackals!

PARMENION: And yours. Oh no. Let's not start it again.

EANNA: A wolf howling! Let's stop our ears with wax, Parmenion! But it's impossible to live deaf. No, there's no escape. Don't delude me with your private sky. It's a lie. Silence them, if you can! But you can't! You're part of them!

PARMENION: I'm part of them! If you yourself are part of that herd of Persian prostitutes! Look at that voluntary lust hunting!

EANNA: Curse them!

PARMENION: Look! See! And say that we've come here to the paradise of holy virginity and eastern morality in order to introduce universal defloweration! Am I a part of Thales' prayer? Then are you part of . . . them there?

EANNA: Me? Of the Persian prostitutes? (*She quickly shuts the windows.*) Part of them! Me? Parmenion, my darling! What did you say? What did you dare say?

PARMENION: Only what you did. Let's just slap each other's faces . . . with the scourge of the plural.

EANNA: The barbarian serves Hellas, never Hellas serves the barbarian. Oh my mother, because the barbarian is a servant, but Hellas's people are free. Well, be free and go away from here! Get out of here together with Dionysus! Go follow your own god.

PARMENION: I'm going, Eanna. So this is our private peace in the universal bacchanalia. Our private little sky . . .

EANNA: Forgive me. Somebody's playing with us. Playing an ugly game with us. I see Demetrios's sneer. When you move your head, he stretches out for me from behind you. I must forget him and also Kleitos . . . and the soldiers. . . . Also you.

PARMENION: Also me?

EANNA: Also you the conqueror. Don't tell me anything about yourself. About the friend of the world's conqueror. Only about him who was a child in Pella. Patroklos, toy enemy below a toy Troy.

PARMENION: From the two black horses we laughed with each other . . .

(From outside, sounds of shouting, trumpets, fighting, then DEMETRIOS enters. EANNA flees instinctively to PARMENION.)

DEMETRIOS: In sweet intimacy together. And our Lord is waiting for Betis' surrender.

PARMENION: How did you get in here?

DEMETRIOS: With weapons, my friend. A division of brave young men was enough to take over this louse nest. The whole gang is disarmed.

EANNA: My Father! What happened, Parmenion? You Greeks trapped my father!

DEMETRIOS: Don't ask him. He doesn't know.

PARMENION: What are you doing? Alexander sent me with a peace offer.

DEMETRIOS: But not to dally with the young lady. It's clearly said in Kallisthenes' chronicle: "Betis followed his king on the same day." He didn't come. You didn't bring him. We take him. His public surrender is necessary by all means. And not just anytime. But according to the chronicle . . .

PARMENION: Who assigned you . . .?

DEMETRIOS: Perhaps our Lord. . . . Perhaps just your uncertainty. . . . Your slightly suspicious delay.

PARMENION: And what if Betis doesn't surrender?

DEMETRIOS: On the way we'll convince him—about his own interest. Look here . . . (*DEMETRIOS's Soldiers bring in BETIS tied up.*)

BETIS: Dogs! Rotten back-stabbers!

PARMENION: Free him!

BETIS: Free! You're still playing your role, you lying sonofabitch? So that was your peace offer.

PARMENION: It was what I said!

EANNA: It was, my father. Believe me. . . . O, Parmenion! What have you Greeks done?

DEMETRIOS: Now Betis, you can see that your castle is no longer a castle. Only a favor. Alexander's favor and tolerance. Of course, I thought you were wiser. Now you see, with a snap of the fingers . . . your famous defenders. You should've known that we didn't put a price on your head.

BETIS: But on my surrender.

DEMETRIOS: You're clever, at last!

BETIS: You're wrong, jackal! I remain stupid, duller than the dullest. You won't enjoy my surrender.

DEMETRIOS: You'll think about it. We'll go away and I won't leave a single soldier of mine in your louse nest. Let it remain the Betis Castle of permitted resistance until Betis publicly makes obeisance at the feet of our Lord and makes a declaration to his people. If there remain any . . .

BETIS: There are and there will be! But they'll respond to a different call. Others will come after me; the number of troglodytes is infinite; don't hope you jackal; I'm not the last Betis . . .

DEMETRIOS: Take him away!

BETIS (*while he's being dragged out*): I'm not the last one. Maybe I'm only the first, and you won't be able to count them . . . those whom you can't trap . . .

PARMENION: Stop! Betis did I trap you?

(BETIS glares long at him, then spits in his eye.)

DEMETRIOS: The result of your dalliance. Let's go.

PARMENION: I came alone. I'll leave alone.

DEMETRIOS: As you please. (*Quickly exits.*)

(Long silence.)

EANNA: What have you all done! Oh my God, what have you done! Parmenion, I trusted you and I betrayed my father.

PARMENION: "Trusted?" Even you only "trusted?"

(YOUNG BESSOS enters upset.)

YOUNG BESSOS: I'll send him to the bottomless underworld! Get your head ready, Parmenion! It'll be an ornament next to Darius's, you lying Hellenic dog!

EANNA: Enough of filthy words!

(Persian retainers enter shouting.)

VOICE: Where is the Macedonian jackal! The lousy peace-messenger! Let's quarter him! He trapped Betis. To the gallows with him! Too easy a death for the dirty Hellene, he should be crucified! Let's tear him to pieces!

EANNA: Stop! You're a pack of wolves! A hundred against one? You won't even listen to him?

YOUNG BESSOS: We've already listened to that betrayer!

VOICES: He stole in here like a jackal! Let's put his head into a silk bag! Bessos, don't spare him!

EANNA: Get out of here, all of you!

VOICES: Shut up, you bitch! I bet the Macedonian laid her! She defends her father's murderer!

EANNA: Kill him, but kill me, also. Your own blood! Take his head in a silk bag! But take mine, also! Crucify him, but crucify me also! You brainless, lobotomized—you rabid lunatics!

(Silence)

YOUNG BESSOS: Betrayal can be heard at a long distance, Eanna. Wherever Betis is now, he hears your words. And he'll die without being tied behind the Greek horses. My father killed me, now is the opposite to happen? The child sends the father to his death? I'll look in the eyes of my father . . .

PARMENION: Alexander condemned your father to death.

YOUNG BESSOS: Do you know who my father is?

PARMENION: Darius's murderer, Bessos.

YOUNG BESSOS: It's not true. Your Lord is more perfidious than that. He couldn't have done that. For such a great service . . .

PARMENION: He had dictated a different future for Darius. Not to be beheaded.

YOUNG BESSOS: Hardhearted, terrible, vengeful god! Eanna, what's happening to us? The father shames the son, the daughter disgraces the father. Has a new god been born to us? The power of bribery? Or have we always been his slaves—without knowing it? You can trust only what's born and brought up in front of your eyes because there's always something . . . in the guise of a human being, in the shape of fidelity, while secretly sucking the milk of betrayal somewhere. I couldn't see my father grow up, but you, Eanna, were born and brought up in front of Betis' eyes . . . but that isn't true either. . . . Nothing is true. . . . (*Pointing towards PARMENION.*) The only truth is that he is a betrayer. The double betrayer. He trapped you, also.

EANNA: Mind your father and not me! I'm no one's victim!

VOICES: She also must be destroyed! The bitch as well. All the whores must be quartered! They're selling castle and country in bed! They give everything for a Greek phallos!

EANNA: Have mercy! Together with Parmenion— you'll murder my father, too! He remained in your hands as a hostage. Don't hurt the hostage—you're killing my father, you mindless madmen!

YOUNG BESSOS: Death is our mercy! Defend yourself!

EANNA: Bessos! (*EANNA seizes PARMENION's sword.*)

PARMENION: I'm sorry for you, Bessos, because of your father's betrayal, which you want to revenge on me. Your guards doze, you have no notion of warfare—only your impulsive passion is greater than your stupidity. Betis' castle still stands—you've been deluding yourselves for months and still no one realizes that for Alexander, Betis' public surrender is more important than this mouse hole. That's why I came here alone without intending betrayal and against my conviction. As it is with the Greeks so not all of the Persians are born to be Bessos and I respect Betis for his response. He doesn't surrender. But he'll be dragged behind a horse tied with a rein and will be tortured. I told him that, too. If Betis is the victim of a trap, then so am I. Do whatever you want with me.

EANNA: My father still might be given mercy . . .

YOUNG BESSOS: Some of you, prepare the horses, send a messenger to Suza: if anything happens to Betis, let Zeus-Amon's son get out of bed from beside his concubine and watch Parmenion's victory-march in our public squares.

A VOICE Not with horses! With his drilled ankles he should pull war chariots!

ANOTHER VOICE: A marriage carriage! With the scourge in Eanna's hand. Let us also have a Suza wedding feast!

(Crowd exits.)

YOUNG BESSOS: Can you write, Macedonian?

PARMENION: A little better than you can defend a castle.

YOUNG BESSOS: You shall write to your lord in your own hand: if he still loves you, he'll send us back Betis in exchange for you. If not . . . let Zeus-Amon's son be merciful to you. (*Exits.*)

EANNA: Be merciful to you . . . to us . . .

PARMENION: "Betis followed his King, Darius, on the same day at the cockcrow of dawn, and acknowledged with a reconciled heart his daughter Eanna's marriage to Parmenion: who has withstood so many tests of faith." How cruel is the future, if you desire to touch it even with only a finger—not respecting its secrets. How frighteningly it retaliates when blind ambition declares something to have happened—to be the past—about which the future has not yet decided, and to which, at the most, it allows our dreams to come close. Poor Kallisthenes! He leaves to posterity everything to be corrected. Only appearances and lies in the disguise of truth. Isn't that cruel, Eanna?

EANNA (*hands him writing implements*): Write. The letter. To Alexander.

PARMENION: Yes. (*After a brief uncertainty.*) But to whom shall I write an imploring letter? The playmate of the child Patroklos: he that doesn't exist any longer. The man for whom I undertook the poison test: made me a toy of his caprices. What he became: the god I don't know. Shall I write to an unknown spirit when he, breaking his word, had Betis stolen away? Shall I appeal to him again—by petition? Never again! Neither shall I ever pray again to the gods nor to a god patched up from a human being!

EANNA: Parmenion, my darling. . . . We hardly got to know one another. . . . We barely exchanged a few words by which to recognize each other.

PARMENION: Come torture cart and the scourge in your hand! I won't beg!

EANNA: How fathomless is your disappointment. Lord-God, how measureless! Only your cruelty will be larger if you let my father die throwing him to the ambition of Alexander.

PARMENION: His measureless ambition is that all his words and conjunctions will be realized exactly and in time. No, no, no. . . . Life doesn't conform to his commands any longer . . .

EANNA: Don't you understand? My father has been taken to his death by torture. . . . Parmenion. . . . Life is more important . . . even a bird's life is more important . . .

PARMENION: Is that you who say that? You who were preparing for the forced marriage with poison? Is force more important than life?

EANNA: My father's life. My dear father's . . .

PARMENION: Whether it be that of all the gods, of all the universe, I won't beg any more! Never, never, never again!

CURTAIN

act three

The Suza Palace. The wedding feast in full swing with dancing and singing. The drunken palace guards sing Thales' Prayer. The same song can also be heard from the soldiers' tents outside. The Persians know only the tune of the wedding march. In the corner of the room KALLISTHENES is writing his chronicle.

KLEITOS: Honored guests! (*To the guards.*) And you dogs over there, also. I'd like to raise a toast, but I can speak only about my happiness. Everything happened according to our Lord's will in his vision of the future, and as Kallisthenes eternalized it in his chronicle. About our own happiness I can only say: before his arrival our fate was in the hands of the gods—and of nature. And the gods gave him their power, and nature put her rights into his hands: both the moment of birth and that of death. Because at this dawn in Suza and all over the Empire at his command ten thousand children were conceived . . .

A DRUNKEN VOICE: If we include the twins at least . . . teens . . . teensthousand . . . or even more than . . .

KLEITOS: Of course, twins as well.

A DRUNKEN VOICE: And the triplets . . . Pardon me . . .

KLEITOS: Triplets! And asses like you, too, if our Lord wants it that way. So, my friends, both birth and death are in His hands and no longer in nature's.

DEMETRIOS: Let all of our lives be at Alexander's disposal—forever.

LUSIMAKHOS: Glory to Alexander!

A VOICE: To the universal arranger and reconciler of all.

KLEITOS: Tomorrow already belongs to yesterday! Let Kallisthenes sanctify what has happened. Let's hear him! You've nodded off, old man.

KALLISTHENES: Is it possible to nod off here? In the presence of such history? The Great Suza Wedding Feast with the merrymaking of ten thousand Hellenic bridegrooms and Persian brides . . .

KLEITOS: . . . has fulfilled, etc., etc—we know all that. We're in it. Go on.

KALLISTHENES: Humankind has never had and will never have such a . . .

KLEITOS: . . . happy moment. We know that.

KALLISTHENES: Thales's prayer resounded in unison from the mixed tongues.

DEMETRIOS: Go on and read about the drunks.

KALLISTHENES: Many of the soldiers lost their potency, but Alexander generously forgave them, and then, on the occasion of the dawn survey, he himself made women of those who were still virgins.

LUSIMAKHOS: It has happened. He leaped like a rampant stag to the tents of the impotent. . . . Go on!

KALLISTHENES: As the sign of his surrender, Darius himself appeared having given up . . .

KLEITOS: It has happened.

A VOICE: With a hiatus.

LUSIMAKHOS: Only his trunk was missing from under his head. A trifle. Darius appeared anyway. He came faithfully. Go on!

KALLISTHENES: . . . just as Bessos, who raised his hand against his king, had to quit life for his infidelity. He had to pay for his deed as an example, after Alexander, together with Roxanne, bitterly mourned over the cruelly murdered Darius. We don't want to tread upon Persian honor and we cannot tolerate even the Persians themselves doing it—against themselves. He who survives can avoid neither surrender nor the voluntary acceptance of Alexander's ideas that control the Empire. It is noted with pleasure that Bessos's betrayal was received with indignation not only by Alexander and the governors, but also by his own son, Young Bessos, for which a high office awaits him in our court. We are not going to put a blood price on the head of our enemies, but destructive angst will be all the more persecuted . . .

(BETIS is led in.)

DEMETRIOS: Betis, you heroic resister! So you came according to the far-seeing wisdom of our Lord.

BETIS: I did not come. You brought me.

DEMETRIOS: Still, the merit is His. Read, Kallisthenes!

KALLISTHENES: Betis followed his King, Darius, on the same day at the cockcrow of dawn . . .

DEMETRIOS: Followed—with a little delay. After the cock's . . .

BETIS: Are you deaf? You brought me. You dragged me here.

DEMETRIOS: Human beings are fallible. They have to be helped in wise action. Isn't that right, my Persian brothers? A person's truth lies not in himself, but in his circumstances. Why wouldn't we have helped you to recognize with your slumbering mind the new circumstances? But careful what you say! You came to surrender—and not to mouth off or—God save us!—to revile our Lord.

BETIS: You're not only deaf, but also drunk. I did not come. You brought me here.

DEMETRIOS: And you won't surrender.

BETIS: No!

DEMETRIOS: Aren't you sorry for your drilled ankles?

BETIS: No!

DEMETRIOS: Nor for your one life?

BETIS: No!

DEMETRIOS: Engrave in your mind: you would've come by yourself according to the words of the chronicle. I had you arrested because you wanted to have Parmenion executed.

BETIS: No! But maybe it's exactly that act with which you have had Parmenion killed. If that happened to be in your calculations.

(Sound of running feet. A MESSENGER enters.)

DEMETRIOS: Stop slandering, slave! (*To the MESSENGER.*) What's up?

MESSENGER: I beg leave to report to the governor: an urgent message from Young Bessos. (*He hands over a scroll.*)

DEMETRIOS: Now you see, he's returned to his right mind. (*Reads. He shudders.*) Entertain the guest until I return. (*Exits quickly to the throne room.*)

KLEITOS: Don't die uneducated, Betis. Let's sing to him, my friends!

(*The wedding participants surround BETIS. They sing the wedding march.*)

ALEXANDER'S VOICE: Parmenion! Where are you loitering Patroklos? Hasten to your Achilleus! In his arms is snowy-armed Helen! (*ROXANNE's laughter. As if in echo, women's laughter is heard from the near and distant palace rooms. SUZIA enters all in white. She speaks to everyone in turn, but actually—with the exception of BETIS—she does not recognize anyone.*)

SUZIA: Help me! My uncle, help me! I can't bury him alone! A green lizard is sitting on his eyes. I'm afraid of it. It's sitting motionless on his eyes as if guarding its own dead. My aunt, help me. Let's cover his face. Green flies are buzzing around him, they settle in his open mouth, on his forehead, and on his eyelashes. My sister, help me. Green ants are marching in a long line, they swarm in his ears and on his neck, let's sweep the giant ants off his body! Help me! Green uniformed soldiers cut the rope and said: "The living tree decays from the corpses of betrayers." My aunt, the sun is shining on him, his tongue is dark green, and carrion birds are sitting on the cedar. Green vultures are watching him—his helplessness is appalling. My uncle, don't despise me that I was singing and dancing while he . . . and I didn't hear his screams. All the screams are the same here. He who is joyous and he who is taken out to be hung—all scream the same way. Help me to distinguish the screams. My uncle! (*She recognizes BETIS.*) Betis! Help me to bury my dear father. Take me home, I will burn my green veils. He who is dead is no betrayer, is he?

BETIS: Only pitiable.

KLEITOS: And a cautionary example. On our Lord's order he stays unburied.

SUZIA: Betis, don't leave me alone!

(*DEMETRIOS enters.*)

DEMETRIOS (*Gently*): Suzia! I told you not to get out of bed!

(*SUZIA does not reply.*)

DEMETRIOS: You must rest.

(*SUZIA only stares at him as at a stranger.*)

DEMETRIOS: Come, my darling.

(*SUZIA does not speak.*)

DEMETRIOS: It was our Lord's command. Irrevocable. We must suffer it. We must forget it. The two of us . . .

SUZIA: Alone!

DEMETRIOS: Please, I ask you kindly . . .

SUZIA: Alone!

DEMETRIOS: There are our chambers . . . red wine in our Corinthian beakers . . .

SUZIA: Alone!

DEMETRIOS (*Changing his tone, cynically*): If the gods still like me: you're no longer alone. But with the future little Demetrios.

SUZIA: Alone!

DEMETRIOS: Is that the name you'd give him: "Alone?"

SUZIA: That is what I'll call him: Alone.

DEMETRIOS: Take her with you, Betis. Because you are free. Our armed people will go with you and bring Parmenion. If the smallest harm is done to him, they'll carve you up.

BETIS: Come, Suzia.

KLEITOS: And what are you going to do with your louse-nest castle?

BETIS: I'll collect all the children who are called: Alone. And I'll bring them up—against you! Until then, just go on pursuing me—instead of your revenge with your benevolence.

DEMETRIOS: Perhaps once we'll catch you.

BETIS: Hardly. Because I'm running toward you. Pleasant restlessness to you. (*BETIS and SUZIA exit.*)

LUSIMAKHOS: Persephone! Let Thales' prayer resound! Let's forget what happened! (*He sings the wedding march together with Persephone.*)

*The scene shifts to BETIS's castle. EANNA and
PARMENION are in the same position as in the
previous act.*

EANNA: Now I thank you not only for my life, but
also for my father's.

PARMENION: And whom shall I thank for mine?

EANNA: Alexander's mercy. He clings to you even
more than to his military plans.

PARMENION: I wish I knew why. I'm unable to
follow any longer—his conjurer's tricks.

EANNA: Perhaps two Parmenions live in him. One
of them is Patroklos of Pella, and the other one
is today's rebel. But you see, he forgives this
one, too. You're free, Parmenion!

PARMENION: Freedom. What can that be?

EANNA: "I won't beg! No!"—said someone to me
last night. Perhaps that was freedom.

PARMENION: Could the two of us have enough
space in a short negative word?

EANNA: We'll curl ourselves up small.

PARMENION: Give me back my sword.

EANNA: It doesn't endanger your life any longer—
with senseless resistance. Betis is alive.
Parmenion is free! Glory to the unarmed victor!
The gods be praised that by their grace / I was
not born a supplicant, Hurrah! I was born
Parmenion, Hurrah! This could be our own
Thales' prayer. Under our private sky.

PARMENION: Where is that?

EANNA: You've seen it. You said you did.

PARMENION: I did.

EANNA: And doesn't it exist any longer? Don't you see it any more? You were lying.

PARMENION: I had little faith. I charged him with breaking his word. And I was stupid: I didn't think of Demetrios. I wonder why he hates me?

EANNA: It's not you he hates. But Alexander's confident friend. He who doesn't learn from anything.

PARMENION: Shouldn't I learn from the fact that I charged him with breaking his word—and it's not true?

EANNA: How dumb of me, I was moved seeing your disappointment!

PARMENION: Come with me to Suza.

EANNA: So that you could prove to your lord that, after all, you hadn't disobeyed his command? You'd take me there to do penance?

PARMENION: Only for myself.

EANNA: Into the midst of Kleitos and Demetrios's mocking laughter? Here comes the prodigal son with his assigned woman.

PARMENION: I would cut them down!

EANNA: And the others? (*Sounds of the wedding march.*) And how about this plague?

PARMENION: We'll forbid it.

EANNA: You can't forbid a plague. You can only escape a plague.

PARMENION: Betis's castle still stands because of mercy. Would you escape?

EANNA: No.

PARMENION: After Darius, Betis's surrender was Alexander's greatest ambition. He gave it up for me: can I leave Alexander?

EANNA: Don't leave him. If you still have enough compromise left in you . . .

PARMENION: Don't lecture me! You cursed Persephone, Suzia. Would you revoke your curses?

EANNA: No.

PARMENION: And—would you curse yourself because of me?

EANNA: No.

PARMENION: Haven't I taken away your treasures? Haven't I thrown your gods into the dust?

EANNA: You—have not. You only tolerated it.

PARMENION: So I'm an accomplice. Just keep blaming me!

EANNA: I'm not blaming you. But it always comes to my mind . . .

PARMENION: What happens to us, if we can't forget anything?

EANNA: I don't know. Once . . . still in Suza . . . I dreamt that the white stones along the river grew wings, and they flew up together with the birds. The stones.

PARMENION: The stones.

EANNA: If I still could have that dream.

PARMENION: If it were inhabitable.

EANNA: And it would receive two fugitives. Let's go.

PARMENION: To the east? To the west?

EANNA: If there's no passable road, then it doesn't matter which one you take. (*She's playing again*.) Look, beyond the cedars there's an empty dream. Inhabitable.

PARMENION: Do I see it clearly? Eros is sitting at the window.

EANNA (*Knocks*): Our god Eros. Look! He's looking at us. He's already asking: "who are you two and where do you come from?" "Oh, we don't know. Our old names were left behind together with the dogs' barking. No, we don't know either what happened in Suza, what happened in Athens." "Well, don't you have a memory?" "Oh, our god, your questions are difficult. What's memory? We both know, god, that the stones grew wings and were flying together with the birds. But we don't know what memory is." Can you hear what he says? That we're already happy.

PARMENION: The god of love decided we're happy?

EANNA: He deduced it from the fact of our leaving our memories behind. "But what are the two of you called, you peculiar creatures?"

PARMENION: I'll tell him: "I'm Love, she's Free Will. But we wear our names alternately because the two of us are one." "So at last you've found each other? I know now who you are. Zeus in his great anger split in two the one androgynous human being for assaulting the skies. One half of it became man, the other half woman, and ever since they've been wandering, looking for each other in order to reunite." To us the miracle happened. "Look at us more closely, Eros. All of our little parts can fit together perfectly. We're the rebel whom Zeus split in two."

EANNA: Listen to what he's saying: "all the people ran away out of their dreams, but you went towards them without fear and without memory. Let that uninhabited dream be yours."

PARMENION: Whoosh! Eros flew away. There, his wing glitters, can you see it?

EANNA: Fly, Eros, fly a long way away. On our own we'll populate your gift. We'll sit down here. Do you have a comfortable place, Love?

PARMENION: On Eros's warm place. How about you, Free Will?

EANNA: On Eros's place I'm afraid.

PARMENION: Of me?

EANNA: And of myself.

PARMENION: I thought fear was also left behind somewhere. Don't be afraid of sitting on my lap. (*He draws her to him.*)

EANNA (*Jumps up from his lap*): No, it's not a good place. Memory is stealing back here with Babylonian words.

PARMENION: What does it say?

EANNA: It says:

> O, no! Don't hurt me! Don't touch me yet!
> Let me remain as I am!
> I'm praying to Queen Istar:
> That She love my beloved out of her heart,
> And smite with her curse my destroyers.

PARMENION: Why don't you want what I want?

Rest against me, imploring I implore of

you!
Let the gods measure my thirst.
My heart thirsts after you, dear one!

EANNA: My heart thirsts after you, dear one—and I fear. Why does fear remain, if we forget everything else?

PARMENION: Do not fear what you yourself also want.

EANNA: I fear. Where is total forgetfulness then?

PARMENION: I say again and again I say, and still again, for a third time: Do not fear!

EANNA: Psst! Something slithered past. That was Fear. Perhaps Eros freed it to attack us? The memory left behind was frightening. My father's anger and poor Suzia in Demetrios's bed of desecration. I'll cast a spell on it! I'll destroy violence with potent words.

PARMENION: Say them quickly!

EANNA: I'll shackle you with rope,
      I'll handcuff you with iron.
      God of Fire, you incendiary,
      Dissolve their evil spell!

Miraculous magical words. I don't see Demetrios any longer, I don't hear Thales' prayer. I hear the seashell's ocean roar of the dream house. Come, listen to it . . . here in my ear. Can you hear music? I can. "That she love my beloved out of her heart, / and smite with her curse my destroyers." Thank you, Eros, for your benevolence!

PARMENION: Let me also thank you . . .

EANNA: O, no! Don't hurt me. Don't touch me yet! Let me remain as I am!

PARMENION: Love flutters away if it's startled
    See, mine is poised to flutter away!
    As the bird from the end of the branch,
    So from me my desire parts.

EANNA: O, no! Don't leave me!
    Joyfully I return to my love.
    Even in our sleep we'll embrace each other.
    I long for the one who longs for me.

PARMENION: Like a strong army takes the besieged town
    So I take you to be mine forever,
    So I embrace you victoriously!
    Light struck my eyes, purple and white
    Swarms of butterflies . . . Butterfly-clouds
    Are moving—see—on the horizon.

EANNA: Let your patroness, the goddess help you,
    And with faithfulness in your love bless you!

PARMENION: Let Queen Istar smite with blindness
    Him who doesn't love you

EANNA: With blindness and with sleeplessness—
    As I was smitten with sleeplessness for your love!

PARMENION: Our fate is sealed with a seal . . .

EANNA: I cry incessantly to Nana:
    So that She will protect your love,
    This precious treasure bought at such a high price!

PARMENION: The jealous set themselves upon me: why do I pine after my love?!

EANNA: There are more of them than grass in the meadows,

There are more of them than stars in the heavens.

PARMENION: Let them become silent! Let them perish! . . .
Our fate is sealed with a seal . . .

EANNA: I will stand facing you, my only one!

PARMENION: You are more dear to me than all else!

EANNA: Let the wicked mock us . . .

PARMENION: You are more dear to me than all else!

(SUZIA screams: "Bessos, my dear brother!" YOUNG BESSOS enters. SUZIA follows.)

YOUNG BESSOS: No! We're not going to bury Darius's murderer. Throw him to the dogs!

SUZIA: The gods will smite us. Let's bury him, my brother, I implore you prostrating myself at your feet: let's bury him.

YOUNG BESSOS: No! I won't beg for him! Let him stay where he is!

SUZIA: In death he deserves only pity. He was weak, he fell—have mercy on him. If you'll not relent, at least have mercy on me. Relent towards him.

YOUNG BESSOS: His enemies didn't have mercy on him. Not even for the greatest possible service! Should we have mercy, we whose name he buried forever? Then why didn't you implore Alexander for his life?

SUZIA: I didn't know, I couldn't know. The screams all sound alike . . .

YOUNG BESSOS: From Demetrios's bed—yes! They all sound alike! The concubines are deaf. The concubines don't hear their father's cry for help. The concubines are blind: they don't even see the gallows. . . . It's all silence and darkness in the arms of those bastards!

SUZIA: And don't you think that force exists? Not a drop of understanding in you? . . .

YOUNG BESSOS: Force. Every whore claims that it was force and violence! The evidence that you're lying is that you're alive.

SUZIA: I had no alternative . . .

YOUNG BESSOS: (*grabs her by the hair and drags her to EANNA.*) Do you see this woman? Open your eyes! Do you see Eanna? For her there was an alternative.

PARMENION: Let her go! The alternatives aren't equally distributed!

EANNA: Come, Suzia. You aren't in your right mind. You must rest, come.

SUZIA (*while EANNA leads her off-stage*): Green vultures watch my father—his helplessness is awful. My brother, don't despise me that I was singing and dancing . . . and I didn't hear my father's scream. All the screams sound the same here. He who is joyous and he who is taken out to be hung—all scream the same way. Help me to distinguish the screams . . . (*Both exit.*)

YOUNG BESSOS: The alternatives! And forgetfulness. She forgot her own future, the miserable thing!

PARMENION: And what if she'll remember only from now on?

YOUNG BESSOS: God grant that it be so. Go, Parmenion. Your Lord and friend is expecting you. (*He starts to exit, then returns.*) You're wise, and also gallant. But you'd be even wiser if you were able to do something.

PARMENION: What is that something?

YOUNG BESSOS: To imagine yourself in the skin of the Other—the Others.

PARMENION: Who knows. Perhaps I'm able to . . . and perhaps, that's my crime.

YOUNG BESSOS: It's not me who'll take revenge on you for it. (*Exits quickly.*)

(*EANNA enters, then BETIS who remains in the background.*)

EANNA: Where did Eros go when he left us alone? Where were the two of us, Parmenion?

PARMENION: Where only the two of us can enter.

EANNA: Only Free Will and Love. Our fate is sealed with a red seal this time.

PARMENION: With a red seal.

(*They kiss, then PARMENION exits quickly without seeing BETIS.*)

BETIS: With a black seal, my only daughter, you motherless Eanna O Implacable, terrible, vengeful God! How can we expect help from you when we throw ourselves into annihilation. O, Enlil, gone is our country, gone is the last hope—even the tiniest, personal, little bud-size empire. We have to lop off our own limbs. (*Draws his sword.*)

EANNA: My father . . . have mercy. (*She collapses before BETIS's feet.*)

BETIS: (*gazes at her for a long time then drops his sword*) If only your dead mother could see you now. At least she could see you—our gods have gone blind. Blind narrow-mindedness picks its victims from among our blind gods knocked to the ground. We throw ourselves onto the forehead of violence to become a laurel wreath and we even glorify our mindless sacrifice: free will and love. Our fate is sealed with a black seal.

(*Sudden scene shift. The wild voices of the wedding march. DEMETRIOS dances. KLEITOS dances. LUSIMAKHOS dances. Musicians keep repeating the same part of the wedding march tune until the dancers are dizzy: "I was not born a barbarian, /Not a Persian, no alien. / But a great, immortal Greek! / Hurrah!" KALLISTHENES appears in the throne room door with his locked chronicle book. Shocked silence.*)

DEMETRIOS: Look, my brethren, the knower of tomorrow is shaken.

KLEITOS: Say something, Old Man!

LUSIMAKHOS: What happened at the dawn of the second day?

DEMETRIOS: Open the big book, Old Man.

KALLISTHENES: It's padlocked.

DEMETRIOS: Is your head also? Recite it out of your head! Is your head under a lock, too?

KALLISTHENES: Let it be under a lock rather than—under the earth. After being taken down from the gallows like my predecessor. Because he chattered.

A VOICE: When can we present ourselves before our Lord?

KALLISTHENES: You'll learn when.

A VOICE: We'll march into the throne room singing our wedding march! "I . . . not born a barbarian, / Not a Persian, no alien. / But the great, immortal Greek! / Hurrah!"

(The Muscians begin to play. PHILIPPOS comes from the throne room excitedly.)

PHILIPPOS: Roxanne's command: silence! The Queen's command: All of you are to leave the area before the throne room! (*He returns to the throne room.*)

DEMETRIOS: But what happened?

DOOR GUARD: Governor Demetrios to Alexandros at once!

DEMETRIOS: Yessir! (*Quickly exits.*)

KLEITOS: Again, he's the only one . . .

SECOND DOOR GUARD: Kleitos, Lusimakhos hurry to Alexandros.

KLEITOS and LUSIMAKHOS: Yessir! (*Quickly exit to the throne room.*)

DOOR GUARD: Generals to our Lord!

(The Generals exit to the throne room quickly.)

KALLISTHENES: Let's fulfill Roxanne's command.

(The Crowd exits. KALLISTHENES remains alone on the stage. He stops in front of

*Alexander's bust. After a short trumpet flourish
guards enter and line up in front of the throne
room door. PARMENION enters.)*

PARMENION: Dead silence on the morning after
the wedding. What happened? Did everyone
get drunk? Is everyone asleep beside their new
wives?

KALLISTHENES: Roxanne commanded silence.

PARMENION: Alexander?

KALLISTHENES: Intoxicated. But that's not the
precise phrase. Very intoxicated.

PARMENION: I myself feel like drinking a cup of
wine with him now.

KALLISTHENES: He summoned everyone to go to
him.

PARMENION: Didn't he call me?

KALLISTHENES: Not you.

PARMENION: I'll go anyway . . .

KALLISTHENES: Not yet . . . Why are you late?

PARMENION: I dashed right over.

KALLISTHENES: But why are you late?

PARMENION: I'm late . . . after all, I'm here. A
hostage can't come until exchanged for another.

KALLISTHENES: Your return took longer than
what's allowed.

PARMENION: Do you suspect some secret?

KALLISTHENES: Why are you late?

PARMENION: O! After all, everything happened as
you read it from the chronicle. What happened
tomorrow at dawn? I'll tell you: all the people
ran away out of their dreams. Two of them

went towards their dream without fear or memory. Eros recognized us, and said: let this uninhabited dream be yours. Kallisthenes, my old friend, I act according to our Lord's command. First I refused to obey his command, but Eros intervened—the genuine god of the heart. The real one! He wasn't sanctified by Amon's priests . . .

KALLISTHENES: My god. . . . What are you saying . . . What are you saying?

PARMENION: I'm intoxicated not with wine.

KALLISTHENES: With joy, I'm sure. Alexandros brought you back from a terrible death.

PARMENION: Giving up Betis's castle—his obstinate ambition. What do you say to that? He never made such a sacrifice for me, before.

KALLISTHENES: Apparently the equal of your poison test.

PARMENION: Not apparently! In reality, as well. How long has he been cherishing his plan: Betis's surrender, Betis's call to his people to follow him. Let's admit it would've been a congenial tactical step, and he gave it up for me! For me!

KALLISTHENES: He gave it up. But you shouldn't have been late.

PARMENION: Why? Is he furious? I'll calm him down.

KALLISTHENES: He's not furious. It's something else.

PARMENION: Kallisthenes, you're hiding something. "It's something else." I'm late, so, I'm late. He'll forgive me. Do you know how I'll appease him? (*He picks up the robe from the pedestal.*) I'll put on his robe. The last piece of clothing from his human existence. I'll enter into the holy presence of Zeus-Amon's son on my own behalf and with the symbol of his old self—with the robe of the human Alexander. . . . Well? Wearing it, I'll sing to him my own wedding march: "The gods be praised that by Their Grace / I was not born a supplicant / Hurrah"

KALLISTHENES: "People ran away out of their dreams . . ." that's a confused speech, my son, I'm not used to hearing such things from you.

PARMENION: Because you don't know what happened. You don't know. We stopped using the plural pronoun. We used to say with hatred: "You" and "We." But no more. We've bridged the gap by saying: "You" and "I." Parmenion and Eanna the two in one. I'll take her to Athens, I'll show her the Acropolis. . . . I'll take her to Pella. . . . We'll ramble on horseback oven the grassy places of childhood. . . . I wonder if yellow dandelions still grow there? What's the matter with you, Kallisthenes? You're all a-tremble.

KALLISTHENES: Get away from here! This instant.

PARMENION: Why? What happened?

KALLISTHENES: I've spoken. Get away from here! They mustn't see us together.

PARMENION: I don't understand a word you're saying.

KALLISTHENES: There's terrible trouble. I can't tell you. Get away at once. Go far away. Out of the Empire.

PARMENION: Out of the Empire. That we've created together? For which I've shed my blood?

KALLISTHENES: Horrible danger, Parmenion! Get out now before the door opens. We mustn't be seen together.

PARMENION: Why shouldn't we be seen together?

KALLISTHENES: Don't you understand what I've said?

PARMENION: Your vague hints?

KALLISTHENES: My head's at stake. You're toying with my life . . .

PARMENION: Me?

KALLISTHENES: . . . if you get away too late and we're seen together. I beseech you! Run away!

PARMENION: Speak plainly, or else I'll smash your head and chronicle to pieces. What's in it? What happened tomorrow at sunrise that I don't know?

KALLISTHENES: Modification. By only one word.

PARMENION: "By only one word." Even more obscure. Let me see it!

KALLISTHENES: I can't. Roxanne has the key.

PARMENION: Roxanne . . . What's the word?

KALLISTHENES: Instead of "Parmenion who proved his faithfulness many times . . ."

PARMENION: Instead of? Instead of?

KALLISTHENES: Unfaithfulness.

PARMENION: Let me see it!

KALLISTHENES: I'm telling you . . . but I mustn't read it. Only when pronouncing sentence . . .

PARMENION: Sentence? What sentence?

KALLISTHENES: Death.

PARMENION: Death. (*He laughs.*) Death. How many times already?

KALLISTHENES: I don't know. Run away.

PARMENION: Wine cup, sudden fury, death sentence. And the reasons?

KALLISTHENES: He said, he'd give them in person.

PARMENION: Ah ha! in person. My dimwitted friend. You should've begun with that: in person. I must confess: you nearly frightened me. His death sentences—upon me! If I can still talk to him. Do you know why he does it? He enjoys my arguments even better than wine. He says: tell me, Parmenion, why was I so foolish? As if we were discussing whether we wanted to swim or ride out to Persepolis? You get used to such trifles in his proximity. (*But he gradually loses his certainty.*) You have no idea how quickly he repents his lightning bolts. That's why he never wanted to see anyone after passing sentence. Another personal request for reconsideration . . . you can see him face to face . . . and in living words . . . in a living voice. . . . But I must go to him. . . . He sent a message that I should hurry, because he's expecting me. . . . Here I am. I'm going . . .

KALLISTHENES: Run away!

PARMENION: That's what I'm doing. Only in the opposite direction. To Pella. To Achilleus.

KALLISTHENES: Slave of the past! You prisoner, Patroklos . . .

(*PARMENION is stopped by the guards at the door.*)

PARMENION: I'm Parmenion, you miserable fools! Don't you recognize me? What is this outrageousness? Who gave the order?

CAPTAIN OF THE GUARDS: I beg to report goddess Roxanne through Demetrios.

PARMENION: Goddess?! Are you crazy? Don't you know me? I'm telling you: I'm Parmenion!

CAPTAIN OF THE GUARDS: That's the order, I beg to report, and it includes the name.

PARMENION: You're a sheep! You're deaf! Nobody said anything like that! Let me go or else. . . . Has everyone gone mad in this inferno? Are you all drunk? Take your hands off me, you slave! (*The guards disarm him. PARMENION now in despair.*) Alexander! What's that silence in there? Kallisthenes! What's happening in there?

KALLISTHENES: I don't know.

PARMENION: Did you know about this goddess's order?

KALLISTHENES: No!

(*At the throne room door, DEMETRIOS appears for a moment, looks at PARMENION and KALLISTHENES, then withdraws.*)

PARMENION: Demetrios! You desert jackal!

KALLISTHENES: We're finished, Parmenion! If you flee, I must flee with you. Demetrios will report it. If you go away, I remain here as the secret accomplice of the deserter. History: a state secret that I betrayed. The historian is like a secret policeman and I babbled like a civilian, but how could I have taken it on my conscience. . . . A secret in which your death. . . . I wanted your good—but you've destroyed me with your obstinacy. If I remain here without you . . . it's my death. Don't linger . . . (*He quickly puts his chronicle in front of the statue.*) Let someone else continue it. Servile words, serve everything. The opposite of everything as well. Yesterday always happened the way we wanted it to have happened on the following day. The following day always happened what happened differently. Let someone else do it. There's been no griffin. Nor giants. There was no pity for Darius. Bessos has received blood money from Him. Yes.

PARMENION: Bessos! Gods! Man, ye who enter here . . . ye who enter here . . .

KALLISTHENES: The future will sort itself out. But where's the future? The future is expropriated. Let's go! At the eastern gate. (*Trumpets.*) Now, that prohibits exiting. We're lost, my son.

PARMENION: You aren't lost. Take back your book. You answer for it with your life.

KALLISTHENES: If we both stay then I'm not lost. But you must flee. And then I can't stay. You take out the guards. I'm weak, but you certainly . . .

PARMENION: Kallisthenes, you didn't blab—you don't have to flee and I stay.

KALLISTHENES: Suicide.

PARMENION: I didn't remotely consider fleeing. I await Him.

KALLISTHENES: Even if they knock me out, you're strong. . . . Let's hurry. Achilleus is no longer. . . . Patroklos is no longer. Finished!

PARMENION: I stay!

KALLISTHENES: You've definitely lost your mind.
Then my dear son, Parmenion . . . if I didn't
offend you by suggesting running away . . .
offending your pride . . . then . . . if I didn't hurt
you . . . I ask the gods for mercy . . . for you . . .
(*He picks up his book.*) Change your mind . . .

PARMENION: No!

KALLISTHENES: I'll be the one forced to read it
out loud. You're cruel.

PARMENION: No!

KALLISTHENES: My dear son. . . . My precious
son . . . (*Quickly exits.*)

(*Long silence. PARMENION stands in front of
Alexander's statue.*)

PARMENION: You don't resemble yourself. In gold
and in marble you don't resemble yourself. You
used to work miracles—now the miracles are
made by slaves with and around you. They
deform you with their flattering. These free
slaves—who are even more pathetic than real
slaves—these you despise because you can't
exist without them. But then why did you cling
to me? For the sake of completeness? To garble
together the truth and the lies? How different
you were in Pella. Well, you've forgotten it.
Now whom shall I ask: shall we ever again
drink Macedonian red wine from a Corinthian
chalice? Is that really true— Achilleus? Does he
perish who gets stuck in the past and doesn't
turn his back on his youth? Is the human being
so defenseless—if he arms himself only with his
memories? Son of Zeus-Amon—I confronted

you, I didn't accept Eanna because you ordered her to me from too high up. From the heights where you talked down to your ten thousand soldiers and me: the earth looks small as does the Euphrates with its tiny ripples; the individual and the whole Babel's cacophony disappear. But how could you imagine Eanna with me—together with the horses' reins meant for Betis' ankles? If you're a god, wipe away the memory of Babel's cacophony, but you should know: it's not like our miraculous tree that we saw in the country of the Hindus which grew to be a giant from morning to evening, then disappeared with the sunset. No, it's not like that, let me tell you if that's the reason why you became irrevocably angry with me. I know this down here, Alexander, and I'm telling it to you up there where you see everything and so don't see anything any longer. For instance, the corner of a friend's heart. The shame of a strip-searched girl. The pain of a Young Bessos. . . . I admit: I'm an amateur, I shouldn't have interfered with your intentions—which your slaves call "history" hiding in your strong hands. I was an amateur, and probably stupid as well: I dared to go too close to all that I deemed right, and even worse: I didn't hide it from those in the horserace for your confidence. The secret is dissolving, the relationship is being torn asunder—a bitter lesson, my friend. If you're gracious enough to still talk to me, I'll tell you without being secretive: the tears you shed on Darius's head were not real tears. And there were no griffins. . . . And I'll ask you what you meant by saying that as long as you live, Parmenion lives also. If you allow me. But even if you don't . . .

(In the throne room there is a loud drum roll and then ROXANNE screams.)

ROXANNE: Take me with you, Alexander! *(As if in response to the sound of the drums, from the back of the palace the wedding participants arrive accompanied by the loud sounds of the wedding march. They move in the opposite direction to the Generals who emerge from the throne room carrying the emperor's coffin. The Three Governors accompany ROXANNE behind the coffin. Silence. The procession stops.)*

DEMETRIOS: Zeus-Amon's son, the world's lord, Alexandros died in the prime of his life at the age of thirty-three in the last hour of his wedding feast. He was going today to Babylon to the Island of Dellos to lay the corner stone of a new temple of Dionysus, and to launch Nearkhos's navy to discover new worlds. Alexandros the man died: Zeus Amon's son is stronger and more alive than ever before. His power and its exercise is temporarily taken over by a governing body: Kleitos, Lusimakhos, Demetrios. Before His earthly remains leave this palace, His last written order will be announced. Kallisthenes! Kallisthenes!

KALLISTHENES *(DEMETRIOS hands him the key for the lock and KALLISTHENES opens the chronicle)*: We Alexandros, Zeus-Amon's son, the lawful descendent of the pharaohs, do in our commands and chronicle book modify the word "faithful" to "unfaithful" before Parmenion's name. Because of his several obstinate confrontations, his refusal of his assigned bride, and his publicly declaring false charges against our person and Queen Roxanne, we sentence Parmenion to death by hanging. In order to give him the right of a last word, we grant him an audience. Dated at Suza: June 323.

KLEITOS: Guards!

(The guards seize PARMENION. The crowd starts to form behind the coffin. DEMETRIOS, KLEITOS, and LUSIMAKHOS remain.)

PARMENION *(Takes Alexander's robe in his hands again)*: And the right of the last word that he granted me?

DEMETRIOS: The man who gave it has gone away—now forever.

KLEITOS: And there remains the irrevocable sentence of the immortal Zeus-Amon's son.

LUSIMAKHOS: You can apply to the Queen for mercy.

PARMENION: Never!

DEMETRIOS: But she would also ask: is Alexandros's divinity a dead end?

PARMENION: You're at it.

DEMETRIOS: *(To the guards)*: Take him away!

(The guards lead PARMENION out. KLEITOS, DEMETRIOS, and LUSIMAKHOS follow him. The stage is empty for a few seconds. From a distance comes the sound of the funeral procession drums. KALLISTHENES enters, puts the book down on the statue's pedestal. He collapses into himself. EANNA enters, then BETIS, YOUNG BESSOS, and SUZIA.)

EANNA: Parmenion! Parmenion! Thales's prayer, the wedding march are being carried in a coffin. They're taking them to Babylon. Sir, where's Parmenion?

KALLISTHENES: Parmenion? there . . . that is . . . I don't know. . . . Probably behind Alexander's coffin. . . . But no . . . Parmenion: remains here.

EANNA: "He remains here," merciful gods! All the people ran away out of their dreams, but you went towards them without fear, and without memory. But tell me where can I find him?

(Loud drum roll from close by.)

KALLISTHENES: I don't . . . I don't know, my daughter. All I know is that he wanted to go with you to Pella, to revisit the green grassy places of childhood. And vainly did I warn him. He didn't want to run away. Oh how obstinate . . . gods, how obstinate. . . . I couldn't find the words to convince him. (*He cries.*)

(SUZIA screams. EANNA goes towards the window from where she can look out onto the square.)

EANNA (*sees the gallows*): Gods, my desecrated, overthrown gods! My mother, I didn't know you, now for once talk to me and tell me that it's not true, it's not possible. My father, Suzia, Bessos, tell me that it's not true, it's not possible! Somebody's playing with us, my father, somebody's twisting us around his finger with the cruel indifference of the dead. Somebody is playing with us, but why so cruelly? You don't speak. None of you has a

121

word for me. Who will answer me, my dear father? Who will tell me where we should flee, even from our dreams, my dearest love, you, my faithful Parmenion?

QUICK CURTAIN

A Note on András Sütő

András Sütő (1927-2006), a Transylvanian Hungarian writer, whose name became associated with the fight for individual and collective rights of national minorities in communist Romania, was born into a peasant family in the small Transylvanian village of Pusztakamarás/Cămăraşu, Cluj County, Romania. He studied at the renowned Gábor Bethlen College in Nagyenyed/Aiud and then at the Protestant (Calvinist) High school in Kolozsvár/Cluj-Napoca, where he began writing before starting his studies in directing at the Szentgyörgyi István Theater Academy in the same town. After a short period of time spent in Bucharest as editor of *Falvak Népe* [*Village Folk*], he settled in Marosvásárhely/Târgu-Mureş, where he lived and where he wrote most of his works. Sütő claimed that his duty as a writer was first to be part of the history of Transylvanian Hungarians and second, to tell the stories of this community by highlighting the characteristic features of its people. He was not just a reputed author but an emblematic public figure and an active human rights advocate especially from the 1980s on.

A prolific writer, Sütő wrote a large amount of fiction and numerous plays. Among his most celebrated narrative pieces, *Anyám könnyű álmot ígér* [*Mother Promises a Light Dream*]—published in 1970 as a semi-autobiographical, experimental diary-novel, conceived as a lyrical collage embodying a heterogeneous mixture of official documents, letters, and speeches, together with first-person narrative—became Sütő's signature work of fiction that shone a spotlight on lesser-known issues concerning the Hungarian minority in Romania. This volume, together with the non-fiction *Engedjétek hozzám jönni a szavakat [Let the Words Come to Me]* (1977), was among the first literary works signaling the increasingly problematic situation of ethnic Hungarians living in the hostile political environment created by the nationalist doctrines of Nicolae Ceauşescu's communist dictatorship in Romania. These narratives warned against the regime's evil policies with their tragic consequences including, among many others, the forced cultural assimilation of the Hungarian minority and the progressive elimination of the Hungarian language from education and the overall culture of the country.

Sütő's dramatic works have been essential in preserving the purity of the Hungarian literary language and strengthening the fading voice of the Hungarian-Transylvanian minority. His plays enjoyed an unprecedented success on Transylvanian stages during the 1970s and during the first two years of the 1980s because these performances constituted the most subtle forms of subversive cultural acts. Many of Sütő's works, including *Tékozló szerelem [Prodigal Love]* (1962), *Pompás Gedeon élete, halála és feltámadása [The Life, Death, and Resurrection of Gorgeous Gedeon]* (1967), *Egy lócsiszár virágvasárnapja [The Palm Sunday of a Horse Dealer]* (1974), *Csillag a máglyán [Star at the Stake]* (1975), *Vidám sirató egy bolyongó porszemért [Merry Keening for a Wandering Mote]* (1977), *Káin és Abel [Cain and Abel]* (1979), and *A szuzai mennyegző [The Suza Wedding Feast]* (1981), employed a highly metaphorical language designed to get by the always alert communist censorship and sending signals to all audiences about the deterioration of the Hungarians' situation in Ceauşescu's Romania. Disguised as historical dramas, satires or mythic plays, these works covertly describe the dangers of the assimilationist policies, of forced urbanization and of cultural genocide.

Sütő employed various literary means to unmask the all-pervasive censorship, shedding light on the anti-minority propaganda especially through his dramatic examples. His plays ingeniously describe the sense of perpetual fear induced by the ubiquitous controls of the secret police that led to the eradication of free speech and internal dissent in the darkest decades of the communist regime in Romania. As a result, in 1983 the publication and performances of Sütő's works were banned in his home country. Consequently, his 1980s oeuvre was published only in Hungary.

Despite their success in Hungarian, Sütő's works were rarely translated into English; resulting in only a few English-language performances. For example, three Sütő plays, all translated by Eugene Brogyányi were staged in New York by The Threshold Theater Company and directed by Pamela Caren Billig: the first was *The Palm Sunday of a Horse Dealer* in 1976, followed by *The Star at the Stake* in 1979 and *Cain and Abel* in 1980. Brogyányi's translations later appeared in *Modern International Drama. The Magazine of Contemporary International Drama in Translation*, published by The Max Reinhardt Archive, State University of New York at Binghamton (1980) and in *Drama Contemporary – Hungary. Plays by András Sütő, Géza Páskándi, István Csurka, György Spiró, Mihály Kornis* that appeared also under the title *New Hungarian Drama. Plays by András Sütő,*

Géza Páskándi, István Csurka, György Spiró, Mihály Kornis (Performing Arts Journal Publications, New York and Corvina, Budapest 1991). Years later, Csilla Bertha and Donald E. Morse published their translation of Sütő's *Advent in the Hargita Mountains* in *Silenced Voices. Hungarian Plays from Transylvania* (Dublin: Carysfort Press, 2008).

The Suza Wedding Feast. A Play in Three Acts, translated by Csilla Bertha and Donald E. Morse in 1993, is now published by the AMERICANA eBooks, a division of AMERICANA–E-Journal of American Studies in Hungary.

Réka M. Cristian

Bibliography

Bertha, Csilla and Donald E. Morse. "Introduction: Falling Through the Cracks." In *Silenced Voices. Hungarian Plays from Transylvania.* (Selected and translated into English by Csilla Bertha and Donald E. Morse), Dublin: Carysfort Press Ltd., 2008, 1-18.

Kántor, Lajos and Gusztáv Láng. *Romániai magyar irodalom 1945–1970.* Bukarest: Kriterion, 1971.

Kuszálik, Péter. *Sütő András életműve. Annotált bibliográfia.* Csíkszereda: OSZK-Pro-Print, 2009.

Dávid, Gyula, gen. ed. *Romániai magyar irodalmi lexikon,* Vol. V/1. S–Sz. Kolozsvár-Bukarest: Erdélyi Múzeum Egyesület and Kriterion, 2010, 226–227.